DAY OF
THE FLYING FOX

DAY OF
THE FLYING FOX

The True Story of World War II Pilot Charley Fox

Steve Pitt

A SANDCASTLE BOOK
A MEMBER OF THE DUNDURN GROUP
TORONTO

Editor: Michael Carroll
Design: Erin Mallory
Printer: Marquis

Library and Archives Canada Cataloguing in Publication

Pitt, Steve, 1954-
    Day of the Flying Fox : the true story of World War II pilot Charley Fox / Steve Pitt.

Includes bibliographical references. ISBN 978-1-55002-808-9

    1. Fox, Charley, 1920-. 2. World War, 1939-1945--Personal narratives, Canadian. 3. World War, 1939-1945--Aerial operations, Canadian. 4. Air pilots--Canada--Biography. 5. Rommel, Erwin, 1891-1944. I. Title.

UG626.2.F685P48 2008   940.54'8171   C2008-900392-6

1   2   3   4   5   12   11   10   09   08

We acknowledge the support of the **Canada Council for the Arts** and the **Ontario Arts Council** for our publishing program. We also acknowledge the financial support of the **Government of Canada** through the **Book Publishing Industry Development Program** and **The Association for the Export of Canadian Books**, and the **Government of Ontario** through the **Ontario Book Publishers Tax Credit program**, and the **Ontario Media Development Corporation**.

Care has been taken to trace the ownership of copyright material used in this book. The author and the publisher welcome any information enabling them to rectify any references or credits in subsequent editions.

J. Kirk Howard, President

Printed and bound in Canada.
Printed on recycled paper.

www.dundurn.com

Dundurn Press
3 Church Street, Suite 500
Toronto, Ontario, Canada
M5E 1M2

Gazelle Book Services Limited
White Cross Mills
High Town, Lancaster, England
LA1 4XS

Dundurn Press
2250 Military Road
Tonawanda, NY
U.S.A. 14150

*This book is dedicated to Paul and Bertha Nallanayagam, my parents-in-law,
who have been like a father and mother to me and have always believed in my writing.*

Contents

Acknowledgements

Although writing is a solitary occupation, the research is usually a team effort. Many people assisted me in accumulating the material that eventually became this book, and I thank them all for their help and expertise. In particular I would like to thank Kevin Mah and Lucie Ethier of National Defence Imagery Library Centre, the archivists of Library and Archives Canada, Fiona Smith Hale of the Canadian Aviation Museum, and Second World War RCAF pilots Bill Martin and Leonard Levy for technical information.

I would also like to thank Charley Fox for all his patience with my endless questions. Finally, I would like to thank the waitresses at the Fifth Wheel Truck Stop in Milton, Ontario, for keeping the coffee coming while Charley and I hashed out the details from D-Day to VE Day.

1 The Report Card

In December 1935 a young teenager walked slowly home from school. His name was Charles "Charley" William Fox. Because he was young and he played on nearly every sports team at school, he normally strode down this road quickly, but today he was dragging his feet. He was reluctant to go home because he had just received his report card and, unfortunately, some of his marks weren't good.

"You've got the brains, Charley," his father always told him. "You just don't apply yourself enough."

Charley knew what his dad was talking about. Although Charley rarely found school work difficult, he preferred sports to studying. Sometimes he let his marks drop by playing too much baseball, hockey, or basketball, his favourite. He always promised himself he would study harder "next week," and after that "next week, for sure," but before he knew it the term was over and the marks were in.

Now Charley glanced at his report card and shuddered. His parents wouldn't be pleased. Charley was so worried about his marks that at first he didn't notice an unusual low-toned rumble slowly growing louder.

When he finally did hear the noise, he looked around but couldn't see anything. The roar grew louder and louder until it felt as if the ground under his feet was shaking. Charley turned in time to see three silver biplanes rise majestically over the hill behind him as they followed the road west toward the small city of Guelph.

Aircraft were still a rare sight over rural Ontario, but these planes were especially unusual. Metallic silver, they glowed like shiny spear points in the clear blue sky, and the red, white, and blue roundels of the Royal Air Force were proudly displayed on their sides and wings. Charley didn't know it then, but these planes were British Hawker Furies on a cross-Canada publicity tour.

The Furies were so low that Charley could make out the faces of the pilots in the open cockpits. The airmen wore brown leather helmets and jackets and had big square goggles to protect their eyes from the wind blasting backward from the planes' propeller blades. Charley waved to the speeding aircraft as they passed overhead, and one of the pilots waved back.

FASCINATING FACT
New Then Old: The Hawker Fury

In the 1930s most military airplanes still resembled their First World War ancestors, with two layers of wings, fixed landing gear, open cockpits, wood-and-fabric frames, and no radios. The Hawker Fury was a step toward the next generation of fighters because it is streamlined and has an all-metal construction, and its powerful Rolls-Royce 12-cylinder engine can propel it at a maximum speed of 359 kilometres per hour. But by the time the Fury entered service it was already obsolete, since prototypes of monoplanes with closed cockpits and retractable landing gear were already appearing in Germany, Italy, France, Britain, and the United States. Because the new warplanes could fly faster and higher and stay in the air much longer than biplanes, Britain's Royal Air Force sent most of its Furies to the far corners of the British Empire where they wouldn't likely encounter a modern enemy fighter. Others were sent on goodwill trips around the empire to build support in case Britain went to war with Germany. Many young boys, like Charley Fox, were influenced to join the Royal Canadian Air Force after seeing these impressive, if obsolete, fighters passing overhead like knights on chargers. A few Furies did see action during the Second World War, serving with South Africa's air force against Italy's planes in East Africa where they were used mostly for reconnaissance and ground support. Still, they did manage to down two modern Italian bombers!

As the planes receded from sight, Charley wondered what it would be like to fly. "Don't suppose I'll ever get a chance to find out," he muttered to himself as he resumed the slow trudge down the long dirt road that led to home. He was only a schoolboy in rural Canada with a bad report card, he reminded himself. "The only flying I'll be doing is out to the shed when my folks see my marks."

In April 1939 Charley was still a schoolboy with yet another bad report card, but this one was different. He was in his final year and had failed Latin and French.

FASCINATING FACT
What's in a Symbol?

In the heat of an air battle it is often hard to identify friend or foe as similar airplanes climb, dive, and flash past one another at hundreds of kilometres per hour. As early as the First World War, air forces began using distinctive symbols on the wings and fuselages (sides) of their planes to prevent pilots from mistaking their comrades for enemies, or to keep their aircraft from being shot at by their own ground forces. At the very beginning of the First World War the British tried painting their flag, the Union Jack, on their aircraft, but the many stripes and crosses were only a blur at high speed and the symbol was easily confused with the Iron Cross found on German planes.

The British then opted for a simple red, white, and blue "roundel" like their French allies. This symbol dates back to the Middle Ages when knights wore roundels of various colours on their shields and tunics. The French roundel was based on the revolutionary cockade, a hat badge worn by Patriots during the French Revolution. The cockade was a blue dot surrounded by a white circle and then a red circle.

The roundel used by the British had the same colours as the French one only in reverse order — a red dot surrounded by a white circle, then a blue circle. During the Second World War, the roundels on the upper-wing surfaces of Commonwealth aircraft were simplified to just a red dot on a blue circle. After the Second World War, former British allies such as Canada, Australia, and New Zealand kept British-style roundels on their aircraft, but each country personalized them by turning the centre red dot into a maple leaf, jumping kangaroo, or kiwi bird.

Like the French and British, the Americans adopted a red, white, and blue roundel to mark their aircraft when they entered the First World War in 1917. Their planes carried a five-point white star identical to the ones on the American flag, set on a blue roundel with a red dot in the centre of the star. By the Second World War, the red circle was eliminated because it was thought to be too easy to mistake for the Japanese symbol, a large red dot that stood for the rising sun. For a while American aircraft were clearly marked with a big white star, but then rectangular white wings were added to either side of the roundel to make it more visible. After the Second World War, when confusion with Japanese aircraft was no longer a concern, red returned to the American symbol, this time as a thin stripe in each wing.

The Germans favoured the Iron Cross. Like the roundel, the Iron Cross was originally worn by German knights in medieval times. In early 1918 the Germans adopted the straight-sided Balkan Cross because it was easier to paint on aircraft. The Balkan Cross was used throughout the Second World War, but after Germany surrendered in 1945, the German air force returned to a smaller Iron Cross to distance itself from the Nazi era.

Without those two credits he couldn't earn a high-school diploma and graduate with the rest of his class.

Strangely, instead of getting angry as usual, his father closed the report card with a snap and said calmly, "Well, no more of that nonsense for you then, Charley. If you're not going to study, then you'll have to get a job and earn your keep. Tomorrow morning you'll walk to

A row of Hawker Fury biplanes sits on the ground in Ottawa in 1934. The Fury was a major advance in fighter development, but technology was improving so quickly that it was obsolete as soon as it was produced.

Guelph, find a job, and start paying for your room and food around here. Do I make myself clear?"

"Yes, sir!" Charley answered. He was stunned. Being taken out of school was the last thing he had expected. He thought of his friends in school, and suddenly he missed them. He even almost missed the idea of studying Latin and French. But now his whole world was changing.

Charley knew his father loved him, but William Fox was a no-nonsense fellow. He worked at the local jail as a senior guard. Before that he had served in the British Army during the Boer War. William Fox had come from Ireland, a poor land where most people had to work hard just to make a living. Doing the right thing was very important to Charley's dad.

Up until now life had been easy for Charley. He lived with his parents and two younger brothers in a small town called Arkell. His life revolved around playing sports, quarrelling with his younger brother, Ted, and hanging out with his friends at school where he had been going since he was a small boy. He even had a girlfriend named Helen he was starting to get serious about. By letting his grades slide, though, all that was coming to an end. Charley felt as if a door were slamming shut on the old part of his life. A new life was about to begin, and he wasn't sure he was going to like it.

The next day Charley rose at dawn and walked the five kilometres to Guelph to search for a job. Unfortunately, Canada was still recovering from the Great Depression and lots of men, young and old, were looking for work. With all that competition no one seemed interested in hiring a kid with no high-school diploma or work experience. He was turned down time and time again. Finally, a hardware store offered Charley a job as a stock clerk for 10 cents an hour for a 70-hour work week. Rain or shine, he had to be there when the store opened at 7:00 a.m. and had to stay late each night, then walk home. Of his seven-dollar-a-week salary, three-quarters went to his parents to pay for the food he ate.

Charley no longer had time to play sports with his friends who were still in school. He barely saw Helen except on Sunday when the store was closed. He worked very long hours at the hardware store moving lumber and farm supplies. On the lengthy walks to and from work he wondered if this was the way the rest of his life was going to be.

Photographer: Steve Pitt, Canada Aviation Museum

All military aircraft in the Second World War wore brightly coloured roundels to identify themselves to friendly planes in the air and anti-aircraft crews on the ground. British and Commonwealth airplanes flew with roundels such on this one on their wings and fuselage.

Sometimes he ran into his school friends and listened jealously as they told him about the sports tournaments they were participating in and their plans for going to college or getting good jobs where they could use their brains instead of their strong backs. After a couple of weeks, Charley decided he was going to finish his high-school diploma. His parents were relieved when he announced his intention. Just knowing that things would get better helped Charley through the tough days of work and studying.

While Charley caught up on his French and Latin, though, the world far away was rapidly changing. Across the Atlantic Ocean, Europe was again bracing for war. Only 20 years earlier Germany and its allies (Ottoman Empire, Austro-Hungarian Empire, Bulgaria) had lost a devastating and costly war against the British Empire, France, Italy, Japan, and the United

FASCINATING FACT
The Empire Strikes Back

The Boers were unwilling members of the British Empire. Descended from Dutch colonists who first settled the southern tip of Africa in 1652, the Boers began resenting the British when the latter seized control of the colony in 1795. Many Boers moved far inland to get away from the British, but by the mid-nineteenth century, British colonists and gold prospectors started encroaching on what the Boers considered their territory. The First Boer War broke out in 1880 and resulted in a victory for the Boers after the British government decided it didn't want to waste soldiers and money fighting for a few thousand square kilometres of African farmland. Two semi-independent Boer states were formed — the Orange Free State and the Transvaal Republic.

Unfortunately for the Boers, vast gold deposits were soon discovered within their territories, and suddenly Britain decided that the two Boer republics were worth fighting for. On the pretext of protecting British treasure hunters who had flooded into the Boer lands in search of gold, British soldiers marched into the Boer republics in 1899 and the Second Boer War began.

The majority of the Boers were farmers, but they were rugged, resourceful, and determined to defend what they believed to be their "promised land" given to them by their Christian god. Using modern weapons and guerrilla tactics, they handed the British Army several stunning defeats and appeared to be taking over the entire colony. The regular British Army in 1899 was remarkably small for a force responsible for enforcing British rule. It boasted less than a quarter-million soldiers spread across an empire that occupied one-quarter of the planet with a population of a half-billion people.

When Britain found itself straining to marshal enough troops to put down the Boer rebels, several former colonies volunteered to send men and money to assist the Mother Country. Canada, Australia, and New Zealand all dispatched troops. Although the Boers put up a valiant defence, they were soon overwhelmed by sheer numbers and improved British tactics. They surrendered in 1902, and the Boer republics became British colonies.

Eventually, in 1910, the Boer colonies were merged with the existing British territories in the region to create the Union of South Africa, a self-governing dominion within the empire. The precedent had been set, though. From then on, when Britain went to war, so did the whole British Empire, including South Africa.

States. At the time it was called the Great War because nearly every European and North American nation and many countries around the globe were involved. It was also called the War to End All Wars because people hoped that peace and stability would result once all the issues that had led to the Great War had been settled.

But only a generation later Germany was again threatening to go to war. Germany's chancellor (like a prime minister) was Adolf Hitler, leader of the Nationalsozialistische Deutsche Arbeiterpartei (National Socialist German Workers Party or Nazi Party for short). Hitler was a ruthless Great War veteran who exploited the collective anger Germans felt about losing the war. Many Germans thought they had been betrayed. Their army, they believed, was invincible, but it had been "stabbed in the back" by cowardly politicians, corrupt businessmen, and Communists who wanted to take over the world.

Most Germans felt the Treaty

of Versailles, which the Allies had forced Germany to sign to end the Great War, was humiliating and unfair. Although both sides had started the war, the Germans had been forced to accept the blame for the entire conflict and pay millions of dollars to their former enemies as compensation. Thousands of square kilometres of valuable territory had been taken away from Germany and was given to their former enemies or was used to create new countries. Finally, Germany had to promise never to manufacture modern weapons of war like airplanes or tanks, and the country was only allowed to train a tiny fraction of its population as soldiers. Hitler, whom the Germans called *Der Führer* ("The Leader"), told Germans they must reclaim their national pride and lost territories, even if it meant returning to war, and millions of his people agreed.

At first Hitler and his Nazi Party leaders secretly ignored the treaty. Throughout the early 1930s the Nazis quietly developed tanks and airplanes and trained thousands of soldiers, many more than they were permitted to under the peace treaty. When the Allies noticed Hitler's military build-up, they did nothing. The leaders of Great Britain and France knew their voters still remembered the Great War, and the last thing they wanted was another war, even against a weak Germany. Hitler began modelling his new Germany on Italy, which was run by Benito Mussolini, a former school teacher who had become leader (*Il Duce*) of the Partito Nazionale Fascista or PNF (National Fascist Party), an organization similar to the German Nazi Party. Still, countries such as France, Great Britain, and the United States did nothing.

Hitler made no secret of the fact he planned to rearm Germany and start a war. In fact, in the 1920s he had even written a book about his plans called *Mein Kampf* (*My Struggle*) while he was in jail for trying to violently overthrow the German government. Sadly, not everyone was alarmed when Hitler and his fellow Nazis came to power. Many Western leaders were more frightened by the rise of Communism in Russia because it seemed in danger of spilling over into their own countries. Since the Nazis and the Fascists ruthlessly opposed Communists in Germany and Italy, initially many important people in other Western nations openly expressed admiration for Hitler and Mussolini. In fact, after Mussolini took power for the first time in Italy in 1922, future British Prime Minister Winston Churchill called the Italian dictator "the saviour of his country."

FRIGHTENING FACT
The Luftwaffe — Illegal Air Force

Because the airplane had proved an effective weapon in the First World War, the Germans were forced to disband their mighty German Imperial Army Air Service when they surrendered to the Allies in 1918. The Treaty of Versailles forbade Germany from ever building or buying warplanes again. It also prohibited the training of combat pilots. In 1926, to get around these restrictions, a partnership of German business people and politicians created Lufthansa, one of the world's first commercial airlines.

Under the screen of providing air transportation for civilian passengers across Europe, Lufthansa gave the Germans an excuse to teach pilots in civilian schools. No one seemed to notice that Lufthansa was educating far more pilots than were actually needed for a small airline service. Later, the German military secretly trained pilots in the Soviet Union using the latest Soviet fighters. The German government also encouraged young men and even teenagers to learn to fly gliders since unpowered aircraft weren't banned by the Treaty of Versailles. After a young pilot mastered the art of glider flying, learning to fly a motorized aircraft was a minor step.

When the Nazis came to power in 1933, the German government openly ignored the First World War treaty and began designing and building warplanes. The League of Nations, forerunner of the United Nations, did nothing when Germany officially launched its air force in 1935. It was called the Luftwaffe, which literally means "Air Weapon." In 1936 the Luftwaffe sent several squadrons of planes and thousands of "volunteer" air personnel to Spain to gain combat experience during that country's savage civil war. They flew for Generalissimo Francisco Franco, an ally of Fascist Italy and Nazi Germany.

In a preview of what would happen to the rest of Europe a few years later, modern German fighters swept antiquated enemy planes from the air while German bombers destroyed one Spanish town after the other from the air. Although the League of Nations condemned the deliberate targeting of non-combatants by the Germans, again it did nothing. With the help of his German and Italian allies, Franco's Fascist forces took over Spain in 1939. Not long after, London, Warsaw, Moscow, and many other European cities would suffer similar attacks by German bombers.

By the time the Second World War started in 1939, the Luftwaffe was one of the largest and most modern air forces in the world. Besides superior aircraft, it boasted hundreds of combat-experienced pilots, giving it a decided advantage for the first two years of the war. The Luftwaffe produced many of the top aces in history, and its planes flew from the deserts of Africa to the Arctic Circle. It was disbanded in 1946 after the Allies won the Second World War but was revived in 1955 as part of the North Atlantic Treaty Organization, a defence force formed to protect Western Europe from the threat of an invasion by the Soviet Union and its Eastern European allies. Ironically, many of Germany's top Second World War aces ended up flying Canadian-made F-86 Sabre jets, the American fighter plane inspired by the Messerschmitt Me 262. From 1939 to 1945 the Luftwaffe suffered 485,000 casualties, including 165,045 killed in action.

Fascist/Nazi style associations began forming in all major Western nations. In Canada both English and French Fascist associations based on anti-Semitic, anti-immigrant, and anti-Communist ideology attracted thousands of followers. Members of the National Union Party wore blue shirts in imitation of Hitler's Brown Shirts and Mussolini's Black Shirts, and Adrien Arcand, a leading French-Canadian Fascist, referred to himself as the Canadian Führer. Arcand and many of his fellow Canadian Nazis were arrested and detained after war with Germany broke out. Similar Fascist associations formed in most Western nations, including France, Great Britain, Holland, Norway, Belgium, and the United States.

The American pro-Nazi party, the German American Bund, supported the Friends of the New Germany, an organization that strove to keep the United States out of the war no matter what happened in Europe. In 1939 the Bund held a rally in Madison Square Garden in New York City that attracted 22,000 supporters. Another right-wing, anti-Communist group, the America First Committee, boasted 800,000 members. One of its most famous members was Charles Lindbergh, the handsome American pilot who became a worldwide hero by being the first person to fly solo across the Atlantic Ocean in 1927.

Lindbergh had been sent to Germany by the U.S. government to study Hitler's advances in aviation. When he returned home, he openly expressed admiration for Germany's Luftwaffe and the Nazi leadership. He was even presented in October 1938 with the Order of the German Eagle with Star by Hermann Göring, commander of the Luftwaffe. In 1939, after Hitler invaded Poland, Lindbergh made a controversial speech for the America First Committee in which he urged Britain and France not to go to war with Germany but instead to form a "Western Wall of race and arms which can hold back either a Genghis Khan or the infiltration of inferior blood." By Genghis Khan, he meant the Russian Communists who were invading Poland from that nation's eastern border.

Henry Ford, the American automaker, was another fan of Hitler and the Nazis, and the feeling was mutual. For his service to the German people the industrialist was awarded the Grand Cross of the German Eagle in July 1938. Ford was the only non-German mentioned in *Mein Kampf*, and a photo of the car manufacturer hung in Hitler's office. During the 1930s, Ford invested heavily in Germany's armament industry. Many other big U.S. companies, such as General Motors and Standard Oil, invested in Germany, too, and continued to do business with the Nazis and Fascists until the United States entered the Second World War in December 1941. This investment aided Hitler's ability to wage war. Persecution of the Jews and an unwarranted build-up of the military were no secrets by that time, but like many people of the era, Lindbergh and Ford ignored the alarming aspects of the Fascist/Nazi regimes until it was too late.

Once Hitler had rearmed Germany, he demanded the return of territories that had been taken away after the First World War. Initially, in 1938, the Nazis annexed Austria, a German-speaking nation that had been Germany's ally in the Great War. Although many Austrians opposed the takeover of their country, they were greatly outnumbered by Austrians who welcomed the union because Germany was strong and prosperous again. Hitler was an Austrian himself, and many Germans and Austrians believed they belonged together in one country. Again the governments of France and Britain pretended not to see any danger, so Hitler was able to increase the size and strength of Germany without risking a war.

Hitler's next land grab was the Sudetenland, which was part of Czechoslovakia, a new country that had been created from Austrian territory when the Austro-Hungarian Empire broke up after the First World War. Czechoslovakia contained many different groups of people, including Czechs, Slovaks, and millions of ethnic Germans, who lived in the western part of the country. Hitler now insisted that the Sudetenland be given to Germany, claiming the German Czechoslovaks there were being persecuted by their Slavic neighbours.

This time France and Great Britain protested. Unlike Austrians, most Czechoslovaks didn't want to give up any territory to Germany. The British and French threatened to go to war if German troops marched into Czechoslovakia. But Hitler was

FRIGHTENING FACT
Fans of Fascism Still Out There

Fascism didn't die with Adolf Hitler and Benito Mussolini. In most Western democratic countries where freedom of speech is allowed, associations that openly admire Hitler and espouse the same ideology as the Nazis have risen again. They are mostly small, isolated groups of fanatics who are generally looked on with contempt by their fellow citizens. Few people expect Fascists ever to take power again, but hardly anyone imagined Hitler would one day run Germany when he first began making shrill speeches in the 1920s.

skilled at two things: one, he could make outrageous demands sound reasonable; two, he could often sense if people were actually unwilling to back up their words with actions.

Hitler invited Neville Chamberlain, the prime minister of Britain, and Édouard Daladier, the prime minister of France, to Berlin, Germany's capital, to negotiate what to do about the crisis he himself had created. Ominously, no one from Czechoslovakia was invited. Hitler attempted to charm both Chamberlain and Daladier, pleading that he only sought to liberate the long-suffering German people in the Sudetenland who desperately wanted to be part of Germany. He also promised that the Sudetenland was his last territorial claim. Hitler's friend, Mussolini, helped work out a treaty called the Munich Agreement, which allowed the German army to occupy the Sudetenland immediately. In return the French and British prime ministers could tell their nervous voters that war had been averted. When they returned to their countries, Chamberlain and Daladier were welcomed as heroes. Chamberlain told the British people: "I believe it is peace for our time."

Without British and French support, Czechoslovakia was forced to surrender one-third of its land,

FASCINATING FACT
Sometimes Don't You Hate to Be Right?

Unlike Neville Chamberlain, French Prime Minister Édouard Daladier wasn't convinced by Adolf Hitler's promises that all he wanted was peace. Privately, he told Chamberlain that once Hitler had secured all the oil and food reserves he needed, Germany would attack the West. Unfortunately, Chamberlain believed Hitler, not Daladier. Without Britain's support Daladier was forced to sign the Munich Agreement. When Daladier was cheered by his countrymen as he returned home with Hitler's treaty, he was heard to mutter, "Ah, the fools!"

millions of people, and most of its steel and electrical production. In the east Poland and Hungary grabbed territory, as well. But the world's nations were so relieved that war had been avoided that they barely noticed when Germany invaded and forcibly occupied almost all of Czechoslovakia six months later.

Although the other nations in Europe were relieved that war had been avoided, they were suddenly very aware of Germany's newfound military might. They hastily began rearming and modernizing their military forces, but the Germans had a huge head start. No one was surprised when Hitler next turned his attention on Poland, another country that had been created partly out of German territory after the First World War and partly from Russia. Poland had a narrow strip of land that extended to the Baltic Sea. This Polish territory separated Germany from Danzig, a former German city that had been turned into a mini-country by the same Treaty of Versailles that Hitler and the Germans hated so much. The population of Danzig was 98 percent German-speaking, and that was all Hitler needed to demand that Danzig be returned to Germany, too.

The Polish refused to hand over Danzig because it was the only seaport they could use without passing through foreign territory. The French and British wanted Danzig to stay separate from Germany because it denied Hitler a major harbour that could be used to launch warships. Once again Hitler justified his threats by faking reports that Germans were being mistreated — this time by Poles. Then Germany's Gestapo (secret police) staged several bogus attacks on Germany using German troops dressed like Polish soldiers. In some cases they left behind murdered concentration camp prisoners garbed in Polish army uniforms as "proof" of an attack.

The French and British weren't fooled by Hitler's phony reports and attacks. When German troops invaded Poland on September 1, 1939, Britain and France declared war as they had promised both the Germans and the Polish. What the French and British didn't realize was that Hitler and the Soviet Union's leader, Joseph Stalin, had been holding secret talks and had come up with a plan to invade Poland and divide it between them.

Poland was the first nation in Europe to taste what the Germans called *Blitzkrieg* or Lightning War. Hitler and his generals knew what had gone wrong in the First World War: both sides had become bogged down in trench warfare and had been unable to advance so that millions of men were killed in a four-year stalemate. Tanks, a British invention, had finally broken the deadlock in 1918. To invade Poland the Germans used tanks, coordinated with dive bombers and infantry advancing rapidly in motorized units. The brave, heavily outnumbered Poles were completely overwhelmed when they were invaded by two of the largest armed forces in the world.

As a member of the British Commonwealth, Canada was expected to join Britain in any declaration of war. On September 10, 1939, after a debate in Parliament, Canada officially entered the Second World War. Unfortunately, Canada's military was completely unprepared. The Canadian Army consisted of

FRIGHTENING FACT
The Best of Enemies

Long before Adolf Hitler came to power, he and his fellow Nazis made no secret that they hated Communists. When both groups were struggling for control of Germany, armed gangs of Nazis and Communists fought pitched battles in the streets with knives, clubs, and guns. After the Nazis seized power, they had all known Communists arrested and put into concentration camps. In his book *Mein Kampf*, Hitler wrote that he considered the Soviet Union to be Germany's natural enemy and that when he assumed power he would invade and destroy the country to provide living space for an expanding German empire.

For the Soviet dictator, Joseph Stalin, the feelings were mutual. Stalin sent military aid to help the Spanish government fight Francisco Franco's rebel Fascists and their German and Italian allies. He considered Germany the most dangerous of the Western nations that had threatened the Communist regime in Russia since 1917. And yet, from the early 1930s onward, the Soviets and the Nazis cooperated in military and economic matters. Soviet coal and iron ore flowed into Hitler's factories to make weapons. German pilots and tank crews trained in Soviet camps and lived side by side with Russian troops.

Just before the Second World War, Soviet and German diplomats met secretly to discuss the mutual invasion of Poland. Like two thieves discussing a burglary, it was agreed that Germany would invade from the west while Stalin's Red Army invaded from the east. Poland itself would be divided like a pizza. This alliance of Nazis and Communists completely took the rest of the world by surprise. One of the biggest concerns for Western leaders was the fear that Germany and the Soviet Union would continue to co-operate with each other throughout the war.

Fortunately, in June 1941, Hitler betrayed Stalin by launching a surprise attack against his former ally. Stalin was forced to make a pact with British Prime Minister Winston Churchill. Ironically, these two leaders hated and distrusted each other almost more than they disliked Hitler. Faced with a common enemy, though, they had to collaborate. Between them they stopped Germany from conquering Europe completely, buying time until the Americans, who entered the war in December 1941, could begin making a military impact in 1942.

only 4,500 full-time soldiers and 51,000 half-trained and poorly equipped reservists. The Royal Canadian Navy boasted only six destroyers, which were expected to defend the longest coastline in the world, spanning three oceans. The Royal Canadian Air Force numbered just 4,061 men, including reservists, and its eight regular squadrons and 12 reserve squadrons were scattered from the Atlantic to the Pacific, a distance of about 5,500 kilometres. The RCAF possessed 270 aircraft, but most were training and transport planes, some dating from the early 1920s. To defend all of Canada the RCAF could field only 19 Hurricane fighters and 10 Fairey Battle Bombers, types of aircraft that were already considered past their prime.

But the speed with which Canadians got their military up to strength is one of the most astonishing achievements in the country's history. In just the first month of the Second World War, the Canadian military doubled in size as 58,000 Canadians volunteered for duty. At the beginning of the

FASCINATING FACT
A Country in Uniform

By the end of the Second World War, 1,081,865 Canadians out of a population of 11 million were serving in the military.

war there were no uniforms for the service personnel to wear, no weapons for them to carry, and no barracks to house them. Recruits learned their basic drill in civilian clothes, using brooms and mops for rifles. They slept in makeshift barracks, including stables that had been designed for livestock. But Canadian factories and thousands of tonnes of supplies bought from the United States swiftly transformed Canada into a military camp.

Charley Fox had just finished earning his final two credits on his high-school diploma when Canada declared war on Germany. If not for Hitler, Charley would have been thinking about college or finding a better job. Now his future had only one option: he was going to war!

Many of the local young men from the Guelph area were joining the 16th 43rd Battery, a unit of the Royal Canadian Artillery. Charley's younger brother, Ted, who turned 18 in November 1940, was one of these lads. Charley and Ted were only 19 months apart and, like most brothers, they often bickered and fought over silly things. Charley decided that even if the Canadian Army grew to a million strong, it wouldn't be big enough for two Fox brothers, so he decided to give another branch of the military a try.

Suddenly, the image of those three sleek silver Hawker Furies gracefully cutting through the blue sky like metallic arrows came back to Charley, and he knew he wanted to become a pilot like the men in those beautiful airplanes.

Charley had heard that pilot school standards were high. He was thankful his father had pushed him into finishing high school, but he was concerned that his grades still might not be good enough to qualify. There was only one way to find out. In March 1940, Charley took a bus ride from Guelph to Hamilton, the city where the nearest RCAF recruiting station was located. He joined a long line of other young men waiting to be interviewed. Just like Charley, almost all of them were planning to be pilots. Charley spent most of the day waiting. He lined up to fill in his paperwork. He lined up for a quick physical by the recruiting station doctor. At the end of a gruelling day he was told he was now officially in the air force. Nevertheless, Charley was sent home on indefinite leave because the air force was just beginning to erect the buildings and airfields of what would become the most amazing training program in history.

All summer long Charley and his family listened to daily reports about what was going on in Europe. After Poland fell, nothing seemed to happen on the western border that separated France from Germany. British and French troops sat on one side of the frontier while Germans hunkered down on the other. Comedians dubbed the early part of the Second World War "The Phony War" and the German tactics as "Sitzkrieg," but that all came to an end on May 10, 1940, when German tank units called panzers smashed through Allied defence lines and drove deep into Holland, Belgium, and northern France. Blitzkrieg had begun in the west.

As far as tanks went, the British and French actually had better machines than the Germans and more of them, but they failed to use them effectively. The Allies spread their tanks out in a thin screen across the whole Western Front, while the Germans deployed their tanks in concentrated packs that were able to overwhelm the sparsely distributed Allied tanks. Before the Allies realized what was happening, the fast-moving German divisions encircled their armies and cut them off from their supplies.

One German column was commanded by a dashing division officer named Erwin Rommel, who led his 7th Panzer Division through Belgium, determined to be the first general to reach

THIS IS TO CERTIFY THAT—

No. J 6361 Rank F/Lt.

C W FOX CHARLES WILLIAM

(insert full name in capital letters and underline surname)

whose personal description, photograph and signature appear hereon, is serving in the

ROYAL CANADIAN AIR FORCE

Changes in rank or appointment to commissioned rank are to be indicated below. All entries must be made in ink by an officer. Signatures or initials are not required.

New Rank	Effective Date	Reference of official authority for change in rank and date of authority
P/O	R1-7-41	
F/O	1-2-42	
F/Lt	1-11-44	

Personal description of holder

Height 5' 11½" Build MED.

Colour of eyes HAZEL Colour of hair BROWN

Date of birth 26-2-20

CARD No.1 109236

Signature of holder

Signature of Issuing Officer

Rank F/O Date 5-6-44

Eventually, Charley Fox was issued this identity card by the Royal Canadian Air Force. As a defence against spies and saboteurs, all RCAF personnel were required to carry ID with them at all times.

the English Channel. Rommel drove so fast that he outstripped his supply lines and even radio range. On one day his column advanced more than 300 kilometres into enemy territory. The 7th became known as the Ghost Division because his exasperated commander had no idea where he was. Some swore the 7th Panzer had been wiped out and that Rommel was dead or captured. On June 10, Rommel sent a signal to Berlin that he had reached the French coast. Despite Rommel's recklessness and insubordination, Hitler knew a publicity gem when he saw one. Instead of being court-martialled and shot, Rommel became an instant German celebrity and was promoted.

2 Raw Recruit

Throughout the summer of 1940 the news on Canadian radio about the war in Europe wasn't good. France fell on June 22, barely six weeks after the battle began. The British were in danger of losing their entire army, but Hitler blundered and allowed the Allies to evacuate 338,000 troops from the French port of Dunkirk. Along with the British, thousands of French, Belgian, and Dutch soldiers crossed the English Channel to safety in England. But they left behind more than a million Allied soldiers, including Britain's famous 51st Highland Division, whose men spent nearly six years as prisoners of war. In addition to troops, the Allies lost thousands of tanks, artillery pieces, and vehicles that the Germans later used against them.

With France out of the way, Hitler was free to concentrate all his attention on the last remaining serious enemy in Europe — Great Britain. Canadian servicemen were already arriving in Britain, but it looked as if the war might be over before they had a chance to fight. The British Army had left most of its heavy equipment in France. The Royal Air Force had lost hundreds of front-line fighters and pilots. Just 34 kilometres of water now separated the nearly defenceless British from the seemingly invincible Germans.

Hitler hoped that the mere threat of a German invasion might convince the British to make peace. Winston Churchill had recently replaced Neville Chamberlain as prime minister. Although Churchill had once been an admirer of Mussolini, he was one of the first British politicians to recognize Hitler and the Nazi Party as a menace to all of Europe. When Chamberlain talked appeasement with Hitler, Churchill had advocated rearming Britain's military. But with their military now in shambles, many British politicians, including members of Churchill's own cabinet, urged the new prime minister to make peace with Hitler. Churchill refused. If Hitler wanted Great Britain out of the war, the Germans would have to beat the British in battle. In a radio speech on June 18, 1940, Churchill told his people that "the Battle of France is over. The Battle of Britain is about to begin."

In response the Germans gathered hundreds of barges and boats in ports along the French and Dutch coasts to ferry German troops and equipment across the channel. Tens of thousands of German soldiers were stationed near the coast, ready to board the barges at a moment's notice.

Before the Germany army and navy dared cross the English Channel, though, the Luftwaffe first had to seize command of the air. The German Luftwaffe commander, Hermann Göring, swore that his fighters would sweep the Royal Air Force from the skies in four weeks. After the easy fall of France, the world had every reason to believe him. The Germans had 1,700 bombers and 1,000 fighters that could attack from air bases located from France to Norway. Against this formidable force, the British had 700 fighters, consisting mainly of Hurricanes, some Spitfires, and a few obsolete biplanes called Gladiators. Many German pilots were veterans of the Spanish Civil War, the invasion of Poland, and the Battle of France. Most RAF pilots had no fighting experience except for a handful of veterans who had seen less than six weeks of combat in France. Some novices had fewer than 20 hours of flying in actual fighter planes such as Hurricanes and Spitfires. Many had never fired their guns at a moving target. British anti-aircraft defences had only 1,800 guns of various calibres scattered across the entire island.

But the British had a few advantages. Even before the war they had set up a network of primitive radar stations that enabled the RAF to "scramble" its fighters and have them in the air waiting for the enemy. The Germans failed to realize the importance of radar to the British defensive strategy and neglected to destroy the installations, which allowed the British to get their planes into the sky in time to attack and destroy the enemy.

WORDPLAY

Scramble

Scramble is an air force slang term that describes how fighter pilots rush to their airplanes and get into the sky as quickly as possible. In Britain it is thought to have derived from a rugby expression. When the ball in rugby bounces loose, players run in from all directions trying to catch it. During the Second World War, as soon as a British radar station or ground observer spotted German planes, he or she contacted the Royal Air Force. The airfields nearest to the enemy aircraft were ordered to "Scramble! Scramble! Scramble!" In many cases the pilots were waiting in full uniform and flying gear, ready to rush to their planes at a moment's notice. The aircraft were fully loaded with fuel and ammunition and were started as soon as the order was given. Sometimes, when attack was believed to be imminent, the pilots actually sat in their cockpits with their engines idling as they waited for the order to scramble. In a slightly different context, Americans use a shortened version of the word *scram*, which means "Get out of here!"

The British were also able to replace their lost fighter planes much faster than the Germans. The Nazis were so confident of an easy victory that they didn't increase factory production above peacetime levels, while the British desperately turned every available factory over to war production. As a result, the British turned out 400 brand-new fighters every month, while the Germans could only manage 100.

Although the Germans had more planes and pilots to lose, the British had an edge because the battle was fought over their territory and many of the RAF pilots who were shot down were able to parachute safely to friendly ground while the Germans who were lost over British airspace were either killed or captured. But despite the bravery of the RAF pilots, the Luftwaffe slowly gained the upper hand. For the first weeks of the battle, German bombers targeted British airfields in the south of England, destroying airplanes and landing fields faster than the British could replace them. The RAF was being bled dry. Then a lucky break occurred.

Hitler had personally ordered his bombers to avoid attacking London, but in late August 1940 a German bomber accidentally dropped its payload on the outskirts of the British capital. Britain immediately retaliated by dropping bombs on Berlin.

The British raid on Berlin was ludicrously feeble compared to the tonnes of bombs that were landing on Britain, but the fact that even a single British bomb had hit Berlin so outraged Hitler that he ordered an all-out assault on London. Day and night, German bombers pounded the British capital with everything they could carry. Although many famous London landmarks were destroyed and thousands of innocent civilians were killed, this shift in German tactics saved the RAF from extermination. With their airfields now spared, the British air force was able to repair its damaged runways and scramble its fighters effectively.

FASCINATING FACT
Polished Polish

The highest-scoring Royal Air Force squadron in the Battle of Britain was 303 Squadron, the "Kościuszko" unit, which was comprised of Polish pilots who had survived the fall of their homeland. Although they entered the battle two weeks late, these war-hardened pilots racked up an unmatched score of 126 enemy planes destroyed, 13 probables, and nine damaged. The Polish pilots also introduced the RAF to the more efficient Finger Four flying formation, which greatly improved Allied combat efficiency.

September 15, 1940, is considered the turning point of the Battle of Britain. The German High Command launched more than 1,000 aircraft at London in a massive daylight raid to break the RAF. The British put every fighter they had available into the air, and by the end of the day the Germans had lost more than 60 aircraft against the RAF's 26. It finally dawned on the German High Command that not only was the Luftwaffe unable to destroy the RAF but also that the British were getting stronger each day while the Germans were becoming weaker. Reluctantly, Hitler gave up. The invasion barges that had been assembled in France and Holland were dispersed. The tens of thousands of waiting German soldiers were pulled back from the coast. The Battle of Britain lasted 114 days. The British lost 1,173 aircraft, with 510 pilots killed. The Luftwaffe lost 1,733 aircraft, with 3,368 airmen either killed or captured. More than 30,000 British civilians were killed in the bombing, which became known as "The Blitz."

The bombing of Britain continued well into 1941, but the Germans now limited themselves to night raids over various British cities in England and Scotland. These raids were more of a deadly nuisance than an effective war tactic. The bombs usually missed their military targets and hit civilian homes and businesses instead. The threat of invading Britain was never seriously considered by the Germans again. Had the Luftwaffe managed to defeat the RAF in 1940, Britain almost certainly would have fallen to the German army. It is frightening

FASCINATING FACT
Battle of Britain's Top Ace Was a Foreigner

The top-scoring ace during the Battle of Britain wasn't British, nor did he come from a Commonwealth country such as Canada or Australia. Josef František was in the Czechoslovak air force, but he refused to fly for the Nazis when Germany took over Czechoslovakia completely in 1939. He escaped to Poland and joined the Polish air force. Compared with the mighty Luftwaffe, Poland's air force was tiny and obsolete. When the Germans invaded Poland, František was forced to attack German ground forces by throwing hand grenades from an unarmed training aircraft until he was shot down. He was imprisoned in Romania, but he escaped and made his way to France where it is said he joined the French air force and shot down 11 German aircraft. When France surrendered, František crossed the English Channel and joined the RAF, his fourth air force in two years. In every air force he served in, František was considered ill-disciplined and insubordinate, but he could fly and he could fight. During the Battle of Britain, he piloted a Hurricane and was the RAF's top-scoring ace with 17 confirmed kills and one probable. True to his nature, he refused to fly with his fellow Czechoslovaks and joined 303 Squadron, a Polish unit in the RAF. In October 1940 he was killed in a plane crash. Some people say he was exhausted and crashed while landing; others claim he died stunt flying while trying to impress a new girlfriend. Josef František was the first non-British pilot to win the Distinguished Flying Medal and Bar.

to imagine what evil Hitler could have achieved with all of Western Europe under his control. Winston Churchill summed up the RAF's accomplishment in one magnificent sentence: "Never in the field of human conflict was so much owed by so many to so few."

All through the summer and early fall of 1940, Charley waited impatiently for orders to report for duty. Now, more than ever, he longed to be a fighter pilot. The newspapers, and the newsreels at the local movie theatre, were filled with the exploits of the daring RAF and RCAF pilots who were saving Britain. Canadians were especially thrilled with the deeds of 242 Squadron, an RAF unit of Canadian pilots led by Douglas Bader, a British squadron leader with no legs!

To his relief, Charley's orders finally arrived in early October by way of telegram. He was told to report to Hamilton on the sixteenth and board a special train to Brandon, Manitoba. Charley's family held a small party for him in Arkell the night before he was to leave. His father didn't say much, but Charley hoped he was proud of him. On the morning of October 16, Charley said a quiet goodbye to his family and was driven to Hamilton by his aunt. Only the aunt and Helen, Charley's girlfriend, saw him off at the train station.

The train platform was very crowded. It seemed as if everyone in Canada was taking a train somewhere. There were many young men already in uniform, heading east to board troop

FASCINATING FACT
Handicap? What Handicap?

In 1931 Douglas Bader was an outstanding athlete and student Royal Air Force pilot. Unfortunately, while flying a Bristol Bulldog biplane he attempted a low-altitude slow roll (possibly to show off in front of some visiting friends) and crashed. Doctors managed to save his life, but they had to amputate both of his lower legs, one just above and the other just below the knee. Despite constant pain from his injuries, Bader forced himself to master his new "tin" legs and was soon dancing and golfing, not to mention driving a high-speed sports car that his parents had specially modified for him.

When the Second World War began in 1939, Bader demanded to be allowed to fly again. At first RAF doctors rebuffed his applications, but Bader was determined and Britain was in need of every pilot it could muster. The doctors were poised to wash Bader out of the pilot program at any sign of failure, but the legless recruit topped every course he took. He scored his first victories as a Spitfire pilot during the Battle of France. Because of his skill as a pilot and his mature age (29), he was promoted quickly.

In June 1940 Bader became leader of 242 Squadron, a RAF unit of Canadian pilots flying Hurricanes. When he arrived, 242 Squadron was experiencing low morale due to the mauling it had received in the Battle of France. Bader's war record and personal charisma turned 242 into a fighting squadron again, helping Britain win its desperate battle in the air with Nazi Germany. Flying home from combat, Bader was known to slide back the canopy of his fighter, hold the joystick with one of his tin legs, and light his pipe for an after-combat smoke.

Bader went on to become a wing commander and score 22 enemy aircraft shot down (and one shared kill), making him the fifth-highest-scoring ace in the RAF. His tally would likely have been higher except that he had to bail out of his damaged plane in August 1941 over German-occupied France. Bader himself believed that his Spitfire collided with a Messerschmitt Bf 109. However, there is some evidence that he was either shot down by a German plane or even struck by friendly fire from another RAF fighter. Bader almost died with his aircraft when his right tin leg became caught in the cockpit, but he was able to parachute when the straps holding the leg on broke.

It is thought by some people that Bader's lack of lower legs actually gave him an advantage over other pilots. When pulling heavy G-forces, a pilot's blood drains out of his brain and tries to flow into his lower legs. Because Bader had no lower legs, his blood was forced to stay higher in his body, which kept his brain functioning properly.

The British dropped Bader a new leg by parachute while on a bombing mission over France. The Germans soon regretted Bader's new mobility. As a prisoner of war, he made so many escape attempts that they threatened to confiscate his legs at night. He was finally transferred to Colditz, an infamous "escape-proof" prison where he was held until liberated by American troops in the spring of 1945. With just a few weeks left in the war, Bader's first request was for a Spitfire to return to the battle. His appeal was turned down, and he was sent back to Britain for a hero's welcome. Sir Douglas Bader died in 1982 at the age of 72 with many distinctions, including the Distinguished Service Order and Bar and the Distinguished Flying Cross and Bar.

ships that would take them to Britain. Other young men, still in their civilian clothes, were on their way to military bases across Canada. All around Charley people were crying, mostly mothers and young wives who were keenly aware that this might be the last time they saw their sons and husbands alive. He was glad he had said most of his emotional goodbyes in Arkell.

In the middle of the milling crowd a sergeant in a blue uniform called out names from a clipboard. Suddenly, Charley heard "Fox, Charles!" over the hissing of the train boiler and the hundreds of goodbyes in progress. When Charley answered, the sergeant nodded, made a check mark with a pencil on his clipboard, and motioned with his thumb for Charley to get on the train. With one final round of hugs from Helen and his aunt, Charley climbed aboard, eager to start the greatest adventure of his life.

Up until that time the farthest Charley had ever been from home was Windsor, a small city about 330 kilometres away. Now more than 1,600 kilometres would separate Charley from everything he knew and loved. He had signed up to serve until the war was over, and if the last conflict with Germany was any indication, once he was overseas it could be years before he saw his family again. Although getting wounded or killed was a real possibility, like most young men his

FASCINATING FACT
Bargain Blue

The Royal Canadian Air Force's distinctive blue uniforms are descended from garb worn by the Russian tsar's Cossacks. The Royal Air Force was created in 1918 from a half-dozen independent flying organizations started by the British Army and the Royal Navy. Because many of the ranks and formations of the navy were adopted by the RAF, the official uniform of the British air force was originally supposed to be navy blue, a very dark blue worn by the Royal Navy.

However, members of this new service wanted a distinctively coloured uniform of their own. Fortunately, a British textile company had a warehouse full of military-quality cloth that was azure blue, a colour that resembled a clear blue sky. The cloth had originally been ordered by Imperial Russia for one of its elite cavalry units, but Tsar Nicholas II and his army were overthrown by the Communists in 1917. The cloth was offered to the RAF at a bargain price, and azure blue became the official hue of the new service. When Canada formed its own separate air force in 1924, it adopted the same uniform as the Royal Air Force, as did many other countries in the British Commonwealth. Azure blue is still the colour of the dress uniform worn by Canadian aircrew and the members of many air forces around the world to this day.

age he didn't worry about that. He had never seen a wounded or dead person. Things like that happened to other people, but not to him or even the people he knew.

The conductor signalled all were aboard, the locomotive let off a whistle, and the train bumped and shuddered as it lurched forward. The train first had to travel east from Hamilton to Toronto to pick up more recruits. As they neared Guelph, Charley tried not to look out the window because he knew the train would pass right by his house. He knew his dad was at work, but he didn't want to catch an accidental glimpse of his mother in case it suddenly made him homesick.

Then the train slowed down. For no apparent reason it halted opposite Charley's house. Worried that something might be wrong, Charley walked quickly along the aisle and stepped out onto the back platform of the last car. Standing at the foot of the steps was William Fox in full uniform. As a senior jail guard, Charley's dad was often sent to flag down a passing train to either receive or deliver a prisoner. Today his father was alone. As Charley peered down at his dad, William Fox came to attention without a word and saluted his son. Charley awkwardly came to attention and saluted back. With a proud smile his father waved to the conductor to start the train again.

Charley returned to his seat. Sitting next to him was a large young man who introduced himself as Larry Summers from Simcoe, Ontario. Charley and Larry hit it off right away. They were both interested in sports and both were determined to be Spitfire pilots. They chatted into the evening until it was time to go to bed.

Because the trip would take more than two days, the RCAF had arranged for sleeper cars for the recruits. Sleepers were special cars with dozens of bunk beds built into their walls. Passengers crawled into upper or lower berths and then drew curtains for privacy. Charley and Larry agreed to share upper and lower bunks. Larry wanted the top bunk, which was fine with Charley until they discovered that the upper bunk springs were so weak that Larry's mattress sagged almost on top of Charley's chest. From that night on Charley called Larry "Fat Stuff" because of the way the bunk dipped into Charley's airspace whenever Larry climbed into bed.

Forty-eight hours later the train pulled into Brandon, Manitoba, and Charley, Larry, and the rest of the recruits were immediately plunged into military life. Their first impression was that in the RCAF no one ever seemed to speak normally. Airmen with two or three stripes on their arms shouted at them to form into lines even before they got off the train.

FASCINATING FACT
BCATP — Pilot Factory

Early in the Second World War the British Commonwealth decided that Canada was the ideal place to train pilots and aircrew. The country was safe from enemy attack and there was lots of open space, so there was less chance of hurting innocent bystanders if an airplane crashed. In one of the most incredible organizational accomplishments of the Second World War, the Royal Canadian Air Force opened 74 training schools across Canada in the space of seven months. It was called the British Commonwealth Air Training Plan (BCATP), and its mission was to turn out 3,000 trained aircrew a month.

Canada's industrial resources were strained to the limit as thousands of buildings had to be erected to house, feed, and train the recruits. Across the nation the once peaceful countryside was blasted by the sound of hundreds of bright yellow training planes, known as Yellow Perils, taking to the air. At first civilian instructors from 17 private flying schools in Canada and hundreds of civilian teachers from the United States provided the initial education until enough instructors from the military could be trained. By the end of the war in 1945, there were 250 separate BCATP sites, including more than 100 airfields operating in Canada.

Although Germany and its Fascist allies had a strong advantage in the number of pilots and modern airplanes at their disposal at the start of the war, the BCATP allowed the Allies to soon catch up. There were also flight schools in Australia, South Africa, New Zealand, and even Britain, but more than half of all Commonwealth aircrew were trained in Canada.

By the time the war ended, 131,552 airmen had graduated from the BCATP, including 49,707 pilots, 1,913 flight engineers, 29,963 navigators, 15,673 bombardiers, 18,696 radio operators/air gunners, and 15,700 air gunners. More than half (72,835) were Canadians. The BCATP trained not only pilots for British Commonwealth countries but also hundreds of flyers from France, Czechoslovakia, Belgium, Greece, Norway, the United States, and the Netherlands. To this day a small community near the Toronto Island Airport is known as "Little Norway" because so many Norwegian airmen trained there.

Success came at a high price, though. An average of five trainees a week died in accidents in the BCATP. From 1942 to 1944, 831 airmen were killed.

A few of the recruits made smart remarks only to be told "Silence!" The recruits meekly obeyed. Charley and the rest were then ordered to pick up their suitcases and climb aboard the trucks waiting to take them to the barracks at the Brandon depot. As they drove past some hangars, they caught glimpses of several bright yellow biplanes parked neatly in a row. "Those are Finches," someone said.

"No, they're Moths," another retorted.

Charley didn't care what kind of airplanes they were as long as he got to fly one. The trucks stopped in front of a big brick building, and they were directed off by an airman with two stripes on his arm. The recruits were slightly surprised to learn that their new home wasn't a barracks built to house soldiers but an agricultural building originally designed to house animals.

Again names were yelled out from a clipboard in what was called a roll call. Then they were ordered inside to find their bunks. The agricultural hall smelled of floor polish, fresh paint, disinfectant, and faint whiffs of animal manure. The interior was constructed like an old Roman coliseum with several floors surrounding a huge arena. Their class was told to go to the second floor. Charley and Larry found a stall with two vacant bunks and decided to continue the sleeping arrangement they had started on the train. They barely had time to put down their suitcases when the corporal came back and barked that they had to follow him again.

The first thing they had to do was get an official Royal Canadian Air Force haircut. Several of the recruits had many styles of long hair. Some liked it long on top and short on the sides. Others preferred it long and parted on either side. In the RCAF there was only one haircut — short so that hats stayed on and everyone looked like a cue ball.

For the next two days they heard two things: "Hurry Up" and "Wait" a hundred times. They ran

FASCINATING FACT
Moth Power — Gypsy and Tiger Trainers

Most Canadian and Commonwealth pilots got their first taste of flying behind the controls of two ancient-looking biplanes — the de Havilland Gypsy and Tiger Moths. With their double wings, fabric construction, and open cockpits, both planes appear to be relics from the First World War, but their slow speeds and forgiving flying characteristics make them ideal primary trainers for novice pilots.

The Gypsy and Tiger Moths are two-seater aircraft capable of a modest cruising speed of 140 kilometres per hour. Developed in the 1920s, the Gypsy was cheap, reliable, and easy to fly. It was used to set several world records in long-distance flying, including a solo trip from England to Australia. The Gypsy was marketed as a military training plane, but it only sold in limited numbers because of a major design drawback — the top wing almost completely covers a student pilot's head. That means if a plane gets into trouble it is nearly impossible for the student to bail out!

The Tiger Moth is actually an improved Gypsy Moth. The main difference is that the plane's airframe was strengthened to help the aircraft survive clumsy landings, while the front seat was enhanced so that a student wearing a parachute could bail out easier if required.

Because the Gypsy and Tiger are so easy to fly, they are loved by pilots of all skill levels. When Canadian ace Buzz Beurling wasn't flying combat missions, he piloted his airfield's Tiger Moth trainer, occasionally "buzzing" his commander's office and then landing and pretending that nothing had happened.

The Tiger Moth almost got some fangs. In the darkest days of the Battle of Britain, 350 British Tiger Moths were fitted with bomb racks so they could serve as makeshift bombers. When it seemed as if Britain might be overrun by enemy parachutists the way countries in Continental Europe had been, it was proposed that Tiger Moths be equipped with long scythe-like blades called "paraslashers" that would hang underneath the airplane chassis to slash the parachutes of German paratroopers. Another idea was to furnish Tiger Moths with poison gas canisters and use the aircraft as "human crop dusters."

Nearly 9,000 Tiger Moths were built, with just over 1,500 being manufactured in Canada. The Canadian version includes a sliding canopy to protect flyers from the cold. Once the war was over, Tiger Moths were sold off as military surplus. Many are still flown by civilians to this day.

FASCINATING FACT
The Barber of Brandon

Number 2 Manning Depot in Brandon, Manitoba, is now a museum. One of the barbers who served at the base asked every recruit who got a haircut there to sign a scribbler. He collected more than 22,000 signatures (and a lot of hair). The scribblers are on display in Brandon, and many British Commonwealth Air Training Plan veterans are thrilled to find their signatures in the scribblers.

"at the double" from one room to the next, only to wait in line for half an hour. They were examined again by doctors. They were poked and prodded by dentists. They were issued itchy blue wool uniforms and hats. They were given boots and belts with brass bits that required polishing. To polish the boots and brass they were handed a kit called the "Housewife," with everything from brushes and polish to sewing needles and thread. They were given pillows and blankets for beds that had to be made exactly right every morning as soon as they woke up. Every morning they exercised by running and doing calisthenics to build up their fitness levels. Officially, they were Class 22. Their rank was aircraftman second class, commonly known as an "acey ducey."

Acey duceys were required to memorize hundreds of RCAF rules and regulations such as: "Don't call a sergeant or corporal 'Sir.' Call him by his rank." If you did call a sergeant or corporal "Sir," he would likely growl an answer like "Don't call me 'Sir.' I work for a living."

You called an officer "Sir," but you didn't say anything to him at all unless he said something first. You saluted officers, but not sergeants and corporals. You saluted only with the right hand, while the left one stayed straight at the side with the thumb in line with the seam of the pants. You could only salute if you were wearing a hat and were standing at attention or marching. Hats came off before you entered the mess, which is the military word for a dining room.

In the arena where horses once jumped for shows and cattle were paraded for auction, Charley and his friends learned how to march in formation, which is called drill. Drill is an ancient military custom in which raw recruits are forced to repeat the same movement hundreds of times until it becomes an unconscious action and they no longer have to think about what they are doing. They just do it when the command is given.

To Charley and the other recruits, drills looked easy enough, but they soon discovered that getting 30 people at a time to move, turn, and stop in unison was a lot harder than it seemed. Many recruits became frightened and nervous when they were shouted at by the corporals and sergeants. Some tripped over their own feet. Others forgot the difference between right and left.

Each drill movement, from "Attention" to "About turn," required a recruit to move his hands and feet together and to time his actions so that he performed simultaneously with everyone else. Sometimes the recruits were told to shout "One-two-three-one!" to learn the military rhythm. A few acey duceys muttered about what all this had to do with flying airplanes and fighting Hitler, but not loud enough for the corporal to hear. When their feet began to move as one and their hands all swung in the same direction, the recruits finally started to feel like soldiers.

FASCINATING FACT
Drilling Discipline into Raw Recruits

Nothing says "military" as much as the sight and sound of soldiers marching in perfect unison. It has been proven many times that a handful of well-trained professional soldiers can easily defeat a much larger number of untrained armed amateurs. The ancient Greeks were among the first to employ drill to fight in "phalanxes," which were tightly packed formations of soldiers who locked shields, lowered their spears, and marched in unison as they moved like tanks across a battlefield. This tactic was highly successful against the Persians who were very brave but who had no defence against a solid wall of spears and shields heading toward them. The Romans copied the Greeks with their famous legions, which established one of the greatest empires in the ancient world. In modern times many people have questioned the value of drills, particularly when they have to do them for hours at a time in an era when warriors fly airplanes or drive tanks and don't march on foot with shields and spears. Drills teach soldiers to react automatically to commands, which can save their lives when an enemy attack comes and they don't stop to think about what they should do. All those drills Charley Fox had to endure probably saved his life when he had to abandon his aircraft after it collided with another one in mid-air. Although Charley was barely conscious, he was able to pull back the canopy of his plane, climb out onto the wing, and jump off so that he didn't get hit with the plane's tail. Drill also teaches a soldier to think as part of a larger military unit that is much more effective when everyone works together for a common goal. If you play team sports, you are probably familiar with sports drills. These have been copied from the military because coaches have discovered that teams in which all the players work together to score a goal win more than a team full of good athletes who try to score goals all by themselves.

Besides drills, the new aircraftmen also had many classes to attend. Acey duceys were required to study about ranks and regulations, military discipline, world history, parts of an airplane, and the basic science of what made things fly. They also took turns performing military chores such as cleaning their barracks and shovelling snow.

Sometimes basketball games were organized, and Charley got a chance to show off his athletic skills. Although Charley called Larry Summers Fat Stuff, the big man proved to be a formidable Ping-Pong opponent. Charley could only beat him by using two paddles, one in each hand. Another acey ducey, Walter "Wally" Floody from Toronto, was even better than Charley at basketball. When they had time, Wally and Charley spent hours practising layups and jump shots against each other. Charley was very good, but Wally was always a little better.

FASCINATING FACT
G-Forces and Defying Gravity

If you have ever been in a very fast elevator, car, or amusement park ride, you have experienced G-force, which is the force of acceleration due to gravity. When you are at rest, you are at 1 G, which is your natural weight. If you loop the loop in a fast roller coaster, you may experience as many as 3 Gs, which means that if you normally weigh 100 kilograms, you will feel as if you weigh 300 kilograms due to the force being exerted upon you by your velocity and the direction you are travelling. The human body can withstand a lot of Gs, but only very briefly.

In the Second World War, fighter planes were capable of turning and diving very fast. Some pilots experienced as many as 10 Gs pulling out of a steep dive. This was quite dangerous because even at 2 Gs blood starts to drain out of a pilot's brain. If a flyer experiences multiple Gs for several seconds, eventually he or she will become unconscious and the airplane could crash. Fighter pilots in the Second World War practised making tight turns to become familiar with how suddenly they could manoeuvre without passing out. Knowing their limits could save their lives in a dogfight.

Reputedly, the highest known G-force survived by a human being was an incredible 214 Gs experienced by Kenny Bräck, the Swedish race car driver. In 2003 when the Formula One car Bräck was driving at more than 330 kilometres per hour struck a steel-beamed wall head on, he came to a dead stop in a fraction of a second. Although he broke a lot of bones, Bräck was saved by his helmet and safety harness and lived to race again.

At the end of a long day there were endless chores for the recruits such as polishing boots, ironing uniforms, and brightening up the little bits of brass attached to their hats and belt buckles. One tarnished badge or wrinkled pant leg could land a recruit in a whole lot of trouble during the next morning's inspection.

With all the work and exercise they had to do, the aircraftmen had no trouble sleeping. In fact, it often seemed as if they had just closed their eyes when the lights came back on at five in the morning and the sergeant was shouting again. Charley often thought about his parents back home, or about Helen, but most of the time he concentrated on his studies.

For the first time in his life Charley tried to be the top student. He knew the only way to stay in the pilot stream was to get high marks in every class, so he listened carefully when the instructors talked. Painstakingly, he took detailed notes, which he reviewed every night on his bunk under the bulge of Fat Stuff's bum. There were so many ways to be eliminated from pilot training. The doctors screened everyone for balance and colour vision. If a recruit couldn't stand on one foot for 10 seconds or tell blue from green, he was eliminated. Good physical strength was required because flying put severe stresses on the human body that only the strongest could endure.

Charley was determined to do whatever it took, though, to succeed as a pilot, no matter how hard things got.

3 First Flight

After 10 weeks, Charley's class graduated from basic training. Because the Initial Training School (ITS) was full, the class was assigned to guard duty at Rivers, Manitoba, where a navigation school was being carved out of farmland. It was a tough assignment because winter had now set in and Charley and his companions had to stand in front of a barbed wire fence at 20 below zero with the wind blowing fine particles of snow into their faces. The base was so new that there still wasn't an indoor toilet for the men to use.

In the cramped barracks Charley caught a fever, but there wasn't even a doctor on the base, only a medical corporal who could only give him Aspirin for his headaches. The fever turned into dysentery. Charley didn't mind the guard duty as much as having to trudge to the ice-cold outhouse dozens of times a day while he was sick. Fortunately, it was a short assignment, and soon Charley, Larry, and Wally were transferred to the ITS at Regina, Saskatchewan. The accommodations improved because in Regina they stayed at the Royal Canadian Mounted Police College.

ITS was where many of the pilot hopefuls were eliminated due to the high demands of the course load. They had to master basic navigation using a map, a compass, and a series of mathematical formulas that had to be memorized. They had to learn how to tap out at least eight words a minute in Morse code. They were also taught weaponry, mathematics, radio operation, and friend-or-foe aircraft recognition and basic airmanship.

The classes got smaller as candidates were eliminated by their marks and posted to other military trades such as aircraft maintenance, gunnery, navigation, and radio operation. Ironically, scoring too high in mathematics could also eliminate a recruit from the pilot stream. Navigation was such an important job that recruits skilled at mathematics were transferred to navigators' school, often against their wishes. Excellent navigators were important to bomber crews because the lives of an entire airplane crew and sometimes even a whole squadron depended on their skill to get to the target and back.

Week by week Charley passed every test, but the one thing that truly concerned him was a machine called the Link Trainer. The Link looked like a harmless amusement park ride. It was shaped like a cartoon airplane with stubby little wings, a dinky tail, and a seat just big enough for a grown man to sit in. Wind generators and other devices made the Link feel and sound as if it were really flying. The Link tilted up and down and side to side and spun around, depending on how the controls inside were manipulated. Mastering the Link was difficult enough when the cockpit was open, but to make the experience harder and to simulate night flying a box was fitted over the cockpit so that trainees were completely in the dark.

FASCINATING FACT
Crash and Learn with the Link

The Link flight simulator was named after its inventor, Edwin Albert Link (1904–1981), who developed it in the late 1920s and early 1930s. Link's family was in the pipe organ business. These large musical instruments relied on electric bellows and hundreds of valves to operate. Link became an avid amateur pilot in the 1920s, but the high cost and danger of training novice pilots in real planes convinced him there was a market for a flight simulator. His knowledge of pumps and valves inspired him to build a machine that used air pressure to tip itself up and down and side to side in a realistic manner so that a trainee could master the basics of aircraft controls without the danger of actually flying.

The controls inside the Link Trainer are identical to a real plane's, and the instrument gauges adjust themselves to reflect a pilot's movements so that if he or she "flies" too low or slowly the simulator will "crash." The Link Trainer comes with a box-like cover that mimics flying at night or in bad weather. In the 1930s and 1940s, Link-trained pilots learned to depend on their instruments so that they could fly when bad weather or poor light grounded other pilots.

In 1934 Link Trainers were purchased by the U.S. Army Air Corps after 12 of its pilots were killed in a 78-day period. Other nations, including Germany and Japan, also bought Link flight simulators for their fledgling air forces. By the end of the Second World War, thousands of Links were in use and more than a half-million pilots on both sides of the conflict had started their flying careers behind the controls of the simulator.

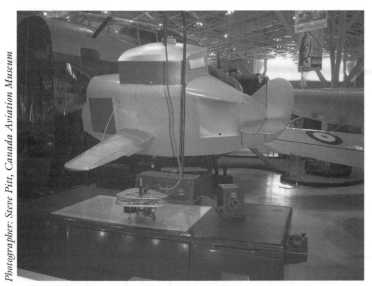

The Link Trainer was a no-risk way to test a pilot candidate's basic flying skills and was also used to upgrade advanced skills such as instrument flying.

From outside the Link instructors told trainees to make a series of semi-complicated manoeuvres to test their skill at controlling the machine and also their ability to remain calm while under stress. Many recruits with perfect vision and good physical strength were unable to keep the Link balanced when the lights were out, or they panicked when the instructors deliberately tried to confuse them.

Charley found the Link test very demanding, but his balance didn't desert him when the lid went over him. Able to stay cool when his instructors barked orders at him through his earphones, he emerged from the darkened cockpit sweaty and a little dazed by the sudden glare of light. But as soon as he heard that he had passed he was overjoyed. Charley faced many more challenging tests in the ensuing months, but the ordeal in the Link was the one and only time he was really worried about being eliminated.

ITS was gruelling but mercifully short. After four intense weeks, Charley, Larry, and Wally were told they had passed and were now promoted to leading airmen. The promotion meant a raise in pay from $1 to $1.10 a day. Charley felt rich. With all his expenses already paid he now had more than $30 a month for just spending money. Leading airmen were also entitled to insert a little white triangle of cloth called a "flash" in their wedge-shaped service hats. The flash indicated they were aircrew in training.

Charley had been in the RCAF only three months so far, but he had already been stationed at three bases in two provinces. Not surprisingly, when it was time for Charley to attend

Elementary Flying Training School (EFTS), he was transferred again, this time to Mount Hope, Ontario. Mount Hope was on the outskirts of Hamilton, so Charley, Larry, and Wally found themselves right back where they had started.

At Number 10 Elementary Flight Training School, Charley and his classmates returned to the books. Now, before they even got to sit in a real cockpit, they had to understand how an airplane's controls worked.

With a few exceptions, from the First World War to the present day, the majority of airplanes have used exactly the same "control surfaces" to determine the direction an aircraft goes. On the back surface of each wing is an aileron, which literally means "little wing." Before Orville and Wilbur Wright developed their first successful heavier-than-air flying machines, they spent hours looking skyward to study seagulls as the birds swirled effortlessly on the wind currents without flapping their wings. The Wright brothers noticed that to change direction the gulls merely tipped the feathers on their wings up on one side and down on the other. This action produced a difference in air pressure on either side, which turned the gulls in the direction they wanted to go. The Wright brothers imitated this movement in their very first machines, but they came up with a complicated system that actually

WORDPLAY

Joystick

Thanks to the popularity of computer games, joysticks are now a common sight in many households. At one time, though, joysticks were almost exclusively found in airplanes. There are many explanations of how the joystick got its peculiar name. Some people take a "poetical" stance, explaining that a joystick controls a plane's ailerons and elevators. Pulling back on the stick makes the aircraft leave the ground and thus the stick delivers the joy of flying. Other people take the historical approach. In the nineteenth century an American riverboat pilot and inventor named James Henry Joyce patented a device for steering boats. Instead of the traditional pilot wheel it was a single stick that could be tilted forward, backward, and side to side. It was known as a Joyce Stick, which possibly became *joystick*. We will probably never know the exact origin of the word, but joysticks are now the controller of choice from the National Aeronautics and Space Administration (NASA) Space Shuttle to the *Queen Elizabeth 2* ocean liner, not to mention millions of couch potatoes playing their favourite video game.

warped both wings of their planes. Eventually, other air pioneers such as Alexander Graham Bell in Canada and Robert Esnault-Pelterie in France discovered that the whole wing didn't have to be warped to make an aircraft turn. All that was required was a small, hinged flap mounted on the back of each wing, which was controlled by a cable connected to the joystick. When the pilot twisted the joystick to the left, the aileron on the left wing dropped and the aileron on the right wing rose. This action forced the airplane to tilt to the left, which caused the craft to turn in that direction. The opposite happened when the pilot tipped the joystick to the right.

The aileron works together with two other control surfaces on the back of the plane. On the tail of an airplane are the elevators and the rudder. The elevators resemble the ailerons in that they are horizontal flaps on the back of small wings mounted on the tail. When the joystick is tilted forward, the elevators are lowered. Pulling the joystick back makes the elevators rise. When the plane is moving very fast, the air rushing over the elevators points the tail of the craft up or down, depending on how the pilot pulls or pushes the joystick. The ailerons are also connected to the joystick. When the pilot pulls the joystick back, both ailerons tip up. When the joystick is pushed straight forward, they point down. The ailerons, together with the tail, can easily make the airplane climb or descend.

The rudder is just like a boat rudder only upside down — it usually sticks up at the back of the plane instead of down as it does on a boat. It is controlled by two pedals on the floor of the cockpit. If a pilot steps on the right pedal, the rudder turns to the right, which makes the plane turn right. The opposite happens if the pilot steps on the left pedal.

Part of the challenge of flying an airplane is to learn to use all three control surfaces simultaneously. The rudder moves an airplane left or right, but it turns much faster and more gracefully if the pilot also tips the joystick left as he steps down on the left rudder pedal. The tilting wings, combined with the turning rudder, make the airplane shift to the left like a racing car going around a "banked" track, which is why turns like this are called "banking."

If a pilot twists the ailerons too far, however, the airplane can slip or sideslip so that the craft is tilted too far sideways, with one wing pointing straight up and one wing pointing straight down. Because there is no longer any lift under the wings, the aircraft immediately begins to slip downward toward the centre of a turn, or sideways like a crab. If the airplane is high enough off the ground and in the hands of an experienced pilot, this isn't a bad thing. Many pilots use sideslips as a way of reducing altitude quickly while changing direction, which can be a good offensive manoeuvre in combat. But sideslipping is quite dangerous when an airplane is low to the ground and the pilot is inexperienced. An uncontrolled slip can easily lead to a crash.

When a pilot turns the rudder hard without using the ailerons, an airplane can go into a skid. A skid occurs when an airplane tries to go in the same direction it was originally going even though its nose is no longer pointing toward the front. The plane skids away from the centre of a turn the way a car slides sideways on a sheet of ice. Suddenly, the side of the car is pointing forward and the front of the car is pointing sideways. Once again, at high altitude and with an experienced pilot, this isn't a bad thing; it is just one more aerial manoeuvre to be used by a pilot. But in the hands of a novice at low altitude a skid can be fatal because until the plane comes out of a skid the pilot has no real control of his aircraft.

Unlike ground vehicles, aircraft can tip up and down, left and right, and sideways in a seemingly infinite combination of angles. Because the motion of airplanes resembles the movement of boats travelling in rough seas, early flyers borrowed ancient nautical terms to describe the way modern flying machines traverse the skies.

Pitch refers to what angle the aircraft's nose is up or down. Yaw expresses what degree an aircraft's nose turns left or right. Roll conveys the degree an airplane tilts sideways left or right. Rolling automatically affects both the pitch and yaw. When a plane rolls left or right, the pitch and yaw change and the pilot has to compensate with the rudder and elevators to keep the aircraft from falling or climbing. To fly well pilots have to learn how to use their elevators, rudder, and ailerons simultaneously so that their planes go in the right direction instead of slipping, skidding, yawing, or rolling by accident.

As they sat in their room, Class 22 heard the growling of airplane engines outside as students from senior classes took to the air on their first flights. Charley couldn't wait for his initial chance to fly. Then, finally, the day came. Charley was issued a helmet, goggles, heavy gloves, and a padded flight suit to protect him from the cold, something he would really need since his first flight would be on January 5, 1941. The heavy padding also provided some protection from fire and jagged metal, a big danger during flight training.

Charley's instructor was Mr. Brown, a civilian pilot recruited from the United States because of a shortage of qualified teachers in Canada. The first airplane Charley flew was a Fleet Finch. The Finch looked a lot like the Tiger and Gypsy Moth trainers used at other bases. It was a biplane painted bright yellow with two cockpits in tandem. First, Mr. Brown and Charley did a circle inspection of the aircraft to make sure it was airworthy. Although RCAF airplanes were maintained by highly trained professional ground crew, it was the pilots' responsibility to check their airplanes before they took off. Mr. Brown asked Charley a few questions as they moved the rudder and other control surfaces, checked the wing struts, and made certain that the tires were fully inflated and that the tail wheel was fit for takeoff.

Satisfied with the condition of their airplane, Mr. Brown climbed into the back cockpit while Charley carefully clambered into the front. After they did a joint inspection and review of the cockpit and controls, Mr. Brown slid the Plexiglas canopy forward and started the engine. Charley was startled at first by the tremendous racket of the engine snarling to life and the blast of air thrown back by the propeller. Excitement mounting, he watched the throttle move forward and the joystick wobble as if there were a ghost in the cockpit. Then, with Mr.

FASCINATING FACT
Slow Ride in a Fleet Finch

Most of the time in the Second World War Canadians flew in aircraft developed in other countries. The Fleet Finch is the only warplane of the Second World War designed and produced specifically for the Royal Canadian Air Force. Four hundred and thirty-seven Finches were built by the Fleet Aircraft Company of Fort Erie, Ontario. It is a "primary" trainer, meaning it was the first real plane a novice RCAF flyer likely piloted. The Finch is a biplane featuring tandem (one behind the other) cockpits with duplicate controls so that a instructor can take over if a novice loses control of the plane. Constructed of metal, wood, and fabric, the Finch has a sliding canopy to keep its crew warm in the winter. A modest five-cylinder, 125-horsepower radial engine enables the Finch to achieve a maximum speed of 167 kilometres per hour with a cruising velocity of 137 kilometres per hour. At the rate of 132 metres per minute the Finch can climb to a maximum ceiling of 3,000 metres. The Finch was well regarded by the Second World War airmen who used it. It is reliable, rugged, easy to fly, and capable of graceful aerobatics in the hands of a skilled pilot. Finches served at 12 British Commonwealth Air Training Plan bases across Canada until they were replaced later in the war with the Fairchild PT-19 Cornell, a monoplane designed in the United States.

Brown at the controls, the tiny aircraft waddled and bounced toward the main runway. They paused for a moment at the end of the runway while Mr. Brown checked that no other airplanes were taking off or landing at the same time. Then the engine roared as it was given full throttle, and the Finch accelerated down the tarmac. Although the runway was smooth, the Finch shook violently because its small wheels had no shock absorbers to dampen the vibrations.

Up until then the fastest vehicle Charley had been in was a motorcar, but the automobiles of that era rarely exceeded 80 kilometres per hour. The Finch topped 80 and kept accelerating.

Department of National Defence PL-2035

Hundreds of thousands of Allied pilots, including Charley Fox, tasted flight for the first time in the cockpit of the Canadian-made Fleet Finch.

As it hit 115 kilometres per hour, the vibrations suddenly stopped as the airplane's wheels lifted off the ground and Charley felt the thrill of flying for the first time. The airplane rose gracefully through the cold winter sky as the ground fell away behind them. Charley was happy to notice that he wasn't the least bit frightened. In fact, at that moment he knew he was born to be a pilot. When Mr. Brown levelled off at around 1,000 metres, he allowed Charley to try the controls. Charley nudged the joystick left, and the Finch gently sideslipped left. He tilted the joystick right, and the plane repeated the motion in the opposite direction. He tried left rudder, and the nose of the airplane yawed left. It was just as he had studied in class, only this time he was thousands of metres off the ground and hurtling along at a dizzying 140 kilometres per hour!

The Fleet Finch was designed to be an easy-to-fly airplane, and Charley mastered the feel of the controls quickly as he learned to make coordinated rudder/joystick turns and other

FASCINATING FACT
Time of the Ancient Mariners

Officially, aircraft speed is measured in knots, another tradition inherited from Britain's Royal Navy. A nautical mile (1,852 metres) is slightly larger than a land mile (1,609 metres). To determine speed, sailing ships used to throw wedge-shaped wooden chips overboard with ropes attached. For every 14.4 metres of line, there was a knot. Another sailor timed 30 seconds using a sandglass. If four knots passed in 30 seconds, the vessel was travelling at four knots per hour, meaning it was covering four nautical miles in 60 minutes. With precision tools like that the Royal Navy ruled the waves for centuries!

simple manoeuvres. Novice British Commonwealth Air Training Plan (BCATP) pilots started off by flying "bumps and circuits" as a solo test. The "bumps" were practice takeoffs and landings made in the course of doing a circuit around the airfield. Pilots were supposed to take off into the wind, climb to an appropriate altitude, turn, then fly in rectangles until they were able to come back down. They were expected to make their descents into the wind but just touch their planes' wheels to the runway long enough to confirm good landings, then take off again and repeat the procedure until waved in by an instructor.

Many beginner pilots were heavy-handed (and heavy-footed) on the controls. This tendency made the "bumps" real as the Finches slammed hard on the runway when they landed or were made to take off without sufficient speed, causing the planes to bounce like bucking broncos. Fortunately, the Finch was constructed with extra-strong landing gear able to absorb a lot of punishment. Still, it was a teeth-rattling experience for the poor instructors who had to sit through numerous brutal landings each week.

After six hours of flying with Mr. Brown and doing a few bumps and circuits on his own, Charley was given the okay by his instructor to fly cross-country to test his navigation skills. Fighter pilots had to depend on their own navigation skills to get them to targets and home again. Sometimes they relied on their instruments to guide them to a general area, but for more detailed navigation they used landmarks such as major roads, rivers, power lines, and railway tracks. Charley passed all his early solos with such ease that it wasn't long before he got a notion to show off a little.

By air Hamilton wasn't far from Guelph, so the next time Charley was allowed to fly cross-country in the direction of his hometown, he couldn't resist deviating a little from his

FASCINATING FACT
Americans to the Rescue!

When the Second World War began in 1939, the majority of Americans wanted the United States to stay neutral. Some individual Americans, however, believed that if Britain fell to the Nazis, the United States might be next on Adolf Hitler's war agenda, so they decided to get into the fight early. While the United States was still officially neutral, thousands of Americans went to Canada and Britain and volunteered for service.

More than 6,000 Americans joined the Royal Canadian Air Force and more than 900 were trained as pilots for the British Commonwealth Air Training Plan (BCATP). In Britain, Americans were formed into "Eagle Squadrons," with British officers as commanders. In the Battle of Britain, 244 American Spitfire and Hurricane pilots destroyed 73½ German planes at a cost of 77 American and five British pilots killed. In 1942 almost all the American pilots transferred to the U.S. Army Air Forces (the successor to the U.S. Army Air Corps and the precursor of the U.S. Air Force) after their country joined the war.

Many American civilians, like Charley Fox's flight instructor, took temporary jobs with the Canadian military to train Canadian service personnel until the military had enough people to take over. The success of the BCATP wouldn't have been possible without the skills and knowledge acquired from U.S. experts.

Although the United States was officially neutral until December 1941, a great deal of American war *matériel* also made its way into Canada when rules were bent. For example, until Canada had its factories set up to manufacture its own trainer aircraft, American-made Harvards were flown by U.S. pilots from California to the edge of the American-Canadian border. There they were hitched to a team of horses on the Canadian side and pulled across the border where Canadian pilots climbed in and flew them to their designated Canadian airfields.

The Americans also "lent" billions of dollars of war *matériel* to the British, Soviet, Chinese, and Free French governments in the Lend-Lease Program created by U.S. President Franklin D. Roosevelt. He compared the policy to a person lending a garden hose to his neighbour to put out a fire. The deal allowed the American government to get around its neutrality by not selling or giving military equipment to the Allies. Instead the United States was merely lending or leasing it. U.S. goods ranging from washtubs to warships were shipped around the world. The recipient countries agreed to give them back when they were finished with them or, if lost in battle, they would pay for them at very low interest rates. The Americans also received free rent at British military bases in Newfoundland and the Caribbean.

Canada made most of its own war *matériel*, but the Royal Canadian Navy did receive 50 First World War destroyers from the United States. Although the ships were old and obsolete, they played a crucial role in helping to defeat the submarine menace during the war. The Lend-Lease deal enraged many Americans who thought Roosevelt was acting like a dictator by helping the Allies without the approval of the U.S. Congress. Hitler agreed. He cited the Lend-Lease Program as grounds for Germany's declaration of war on the United States after the Japanese attacked Pearl Harbor. Of all the Allies who received massive aid from the United States, only Britain paid back its debt. The British made their last payment on the Lend-Lease Program on December 29, 2006.

scheduled flight plan. Helen, Charley's girlfriend, lived in a house on a street across from Exhibition Park in Guelph. With nearly 40 hours of flying experience under his belt, Charley considered himself an "expert" pilot, so he decided to do a bump on the baseball diamond across from Helen's home. He bumped Exhibition Park, lifted off, then flew low over all the houses on the street, hoping Helen would look out and see him waving. But she didn't. The noise from his engine caused a two-metre-long piece of plaster to fall from the living-room ceiling in a neighbour's home and destroy a coffee table. Charley was wise enough not to attempt a second pass over the street, so no one glimpsed his plane's registration numbers. Later, though, Helen told him that the owner of the damaged house was pretty unhappy about the destruction of his ceiling and furniture.

Having escaped detection for his Guelph detour, Charley passed EFTS and was sent with his class to Service Flying Training School (SFTS). This meant another transfer — this time to Dunnville, Ontario. Now assigned to master monoplanes, Charley, Larry, and Wally continued together in Class 22.

Dunnville, Ontario, is located about 10 kilometres north of Lake Erie. Before the Second World War it was a peaceful farming community known mostly for growing tobacco and tomatoes on the huge, flat fields that had once been the bottom of an ancient glacial lake bed. This open land was perfect for a flying school, so shortly after war was declared an army of construction workers and military personnel descended on Dunnville. Seemingly overnight the former tobacco and tomato fields sprouted a new crop of airplane hangars, maintenance shops, classrooms, and barracks. Then, on November 25, 1940, Royal Canadian Air Force Base Number 6 SFTS Dunnville opened for classes.

Class 22 was given an extended leave for a few weeks while the Dunnville school was prepared for its students. Charley spent his leave at home with his family, then reported for duty at Picton, where he was to be reunited with his class. To his dismay, though, he caught scarlet fever in Picton and was forced to spend four weeks in a military hospital there and two more in a rehabilitation hospital in Toronto while his classmates went on to Dunnville and continued their training. Charley not only fretted about losing contact with Larry, Wally, and his other friends in Class 22 as he fought the fever, but he also agonized about the possibility that he might be washed out of pilot training altogether.

When Charley was pronounced fit for duty again, he joined the next class of novice flyers passing through Dunnville in April 1941. He was now in Class 28. Although he quickly made friends with his new classmates, Charley envied his former colleagues when they graduated from Dunnville on May 21, 1941, especially after every one of them was posted to fighter training ahead of him. Charley sadly said goodbye to Wally and Fat Stuff as they shipped out. He promised them he would join them as soon as he could.

FASCINATING FACT
Go, Yale, Go!

To most people the North American BT-9 Yale looks virtually identical to the Harvard, its younger cousin. Both planes were created by North American Aviation of California. Both planes are dual-control monoplanes with a fixed canopy. The main differences are that the Yale has a less-powerful engine and its front wheels don't retract after takeoff, which makes the Yale slower and less agile than the Harvard. Just before the Second World War the French air force placed an emergency order for Yales, but France fell to the Germans before the planes could be delivered. Canada bought more than 100 surplus Yales and used them as advanced trainers until its Harvards could be delivered.

Determined to catch up with his friends, Charley worked all that much harder in his studies. His father would have been proud to see Charley studying every night and receiving top honours in nearly every class he took. Besides classwork, there were many new flying skills to learn.

Charley first checked out on the BT-9, a monoplane known as the Yale. It cruised at nearly 250 kilometres per hour and had almost twice the ceiling capability of the Finch at about 6,000 metres. Most students took three to four hours to check out on the Yale. It took Charley 12 hours because the instructors were aware that he had recently gotten out of the hospital, so they took things slowly to make sure he was up to speed.

Still, the instructors must have been impressed with Charley's knowledge and dedication. When it was time for him to move up to the more advanced Harvard, they let him do a one-hour ground checkout before letting him take off solo. The North American Harvard, also known as "The Yellow Peril," was an extremely fine aircraft, but its high speed and smaller wing surface made it much more challenging to fly than the Finch or Moth. A daydreaming

Department of National Defence PL-2222

North American Aviation's Yale was another common training aircraft for British Commonwealth Air Training Plan pilots.

pilot could easily be a dead one in a Harvard. As with the Finch and the Yale, however, Charley felt completely at home in the Harvard and was approved to fly solo on his first flight.

At this stage pilots no longer just flew solo. Charley and his classmates now had to learn to fly in formation. Imagine driving down a winding highway in a car moving at more than 160 kilometres per hour. Now envision racing the same highway in a car hurtling at more than 160 kilometres per hour with at least three other vehicles only a metre or so away rushing at the same speed. Then picture all these cars going around corners simultaneously with the car inside the turn slowing down and the car on the outside speeding up to keep the formation tight.

Formation flying was difficult enough in clear weather when the air was smooth and pilots could see one another easily. But BCATP pilots also had to learn to hold formation in clouds because in combat they were expected to advance toward the enemy no matter what was in the way.

Entering a cloud was a disconcerting experience even for an experienced pilot. Visibility plunged to nearly zero. It was often a bumpy ride as warm and cool air masses mingled and caused air pockets, thermals, and downdrafts. Sometimes the clouds stretched for many kilometres. If the weather was cold, rain could pound on the windshield and ice might form on the craft's wings. In such conditions it was easy for pilots to become disoriented and lose their sense of direction. Airmen even had a hard time telling if they were climbing, descending, or still flying level. The only way pilots could stay in formation was to fly by instruments solely.

The Link was the first step in learning how to fly by instruments, but at the Service Flying Training School level student pilots had to fly "under the hood." While an instructor sat in the front of a Harvard, a student climbed in back and a heavy, lightproof cloth hood was fastened over his head and cockpit so that he could only see the airplane's instruments. For the first few times the instructor took the airplane up, but once a safe altitude was reached the instructor handed control over to the student who then proceeded to fly an airplane travelling well over 160 kilometres per hour from the inside of a big cloth bag.

The student not only had to watch his speed and direction on the instruments simultaneously, but also his pitch, altitude, fuel, and horizon. Finally, the pilot had to bring his aircraft down in a controlled descent, using only his navigation skills to find the airfield. Then, during the last hundred metres or so, the instructor took over and landed the plane.

As students became more skilled at flying by instruments, they were even

FASCINATING FACT
North American Harvard — Ivy League of the Air

Once British Commonwealth Air Training Plan pilots had mastered the basics of flying in primary trainers such as the Moth or Finch, they graduated to the Harvard Advanced Trainer. The Harvard (also known as the AT-6 Texan in the United States) was built by North American Aviation, a U.S. aircraft company. It was designed to simulate the characteristics of a front-line fighter plane and is a closed-canopy, low-winged monoplane with retractable landing gear just like the Spitfire and Hurricane. The 600-horsepower, supercharged Pratt & Whitney rotary engine can take the Harvard to a top speed of 335 kilometres per hour. Like all Allied training craft, it was painted bright yellow so that it could be easily seen from the ground and in the air. It was nicknamed "The Yellow Peril" because if a pilot made a mistake it could easily be his last one.

Like the Finch, the Harvard is a two-seater with dual controls. The student sits in the front of the aircraft and the instructor sits in the back. The sturdy Harvard is "overbuilt" to withstand the clumsy handling of novice students as they bump down the runway attempting takeoffs and landings. One of the most distinctive features of the Harvard is the "snarl" it makes while it flies. This is actually a miniature sonic boom caused by the airplane's twin-bladed propeller spinning at near-supersonic speeds. This trait earned the Harvard two other nicknames — Old Growler in the United States and Window Breaker in Britain.

The Canadian version differs from its American cousins in that it has a pipe leading from the engine past the cockpit to serve as a heater for pilots training in the cold Canadian climate. The Harvard could be fitted with two .50 calibre machine guns, rockets, and even bombs for target practice.

More than 21,000 Harvards were produced during the Second World War, with 3,350 of them being built in Canada, making it the most-produced Canadian warplane of the war. Thirty-four countries adopted the Harvard as their trainer, and it is estimated that several hundred thousand pilots earned their wings in such planes. The Harvard was kept in service by the RCAF until 1965, and many civilian-owned Harvards are still flying today. Other Second World War Allied training aircraft included the Yale and the Oxford. All three were named after famous universities.

required to take off "under the hood." To some students hood-flying seemed like an extreme way to wash out promising pilots, but Charley later found that this training saved his life on several occasions when he was forced to fly through kilometres of fog or find his airfield and land in the dark after a combat mission. Because the United States Army Air Forces only bombed in daylight, its pilots didn't usually get the same kind of intense instrument-only training and many of them ran into trouble if they encountered cloudy weather or were forced to land after sunset.

Another part of Class 28's advanced training was to stall and spin their Harvards deliberately, then recover over and over again until the procedure became a drill and they could stall and recover without thinking. A stall and spin was a frightening experience the first time it happened to a novice pilot because the plane was out of control, but it was better to do the routine under the supervision of a flight instructor than to go through a first stall in combat.

There was a saying in the RCAF that if you could fly a Harvard, you could fly anything, and Charley felt completely at home in the Harvard. He wasn't intimidated by the higher speeds and the touchy controls that made some nervous pilots feel as if they were always on the verge of a crash. In July 1941, just nine months after Charley stepped aboard the train in Hamilton as a raw recruit, he graduated second from the top of his class as a full-fledged pilot in the Royal Canadian Air Force. Like the rest of his

WORDPLAY — Stalls and Spins

In the early days of aviation, stalls and spins killed many pilots. A stall is when an airplane's speed reduces so that there is no longer any lift under the wings. Something comparable happens when skateboarders try to climb to the top of a half-tube but don't have enough momentum, so the skateboard stalls halfway up the wall, then starts to fall back down the other way. If a pilot flies too slowly or tries to take off at too steep an angle, the air passing under the wings that provides the lift drops and the plane either slides backward or tips forward into a spin. A spin occurs when there are unequal amounts of lift under each wing so that there is more lift on one side of the aircraft than the other. This causes a plane to "spin" toward the ground like a corkscrew. Until pilots figured out how to regain control, a spin was considered nearly always fatal. Sometime in the middle of the First World War, pilots discovered that if a plane's nose was pushed downward hard enough, the aircraft's speed picked up and lift returned to the wings. Unfortunately, that only worked if the plane was high enough for the pilot to gain control. Low-altitude stalls and spins cause fatalities even today.

classmates, Charley couldn't wait to find out where his next posting would be. The British were now fighting the Germans from Norway to North Africa and the Japanese from India to Australia. He wondered if he would be assigned to the same squadron as Larry or Wally.

When the assignment orders were finally posted, Charley was stunned to discover that all of his hard work to graduate at the top of his class had backfired. The majority of Course 28 received orders to report for fighter plane training, the last stop before being sent overseas to Europe. But the top 10 pilots were told they were staying in Dunnville because their grades and flying skills were so good that the RCAF had decided they would be better employed in the war effort as flying instructors. One of Charley's classmates tried to refuse the orders and was given a blunt choice: accept the flying instructor assignment or lose his wings and be sent to gunnery school as an aircraftman. Charley and his friends knew they would have to be instructors or they would never fly an airplane again.

FASCINATING FACT
Instructors Get No Respect

As the British Commonwealth Air Training Plan (BCATP) began turning out hundreds of pilots, its organizers wanted to stop relying on civilian flying instructors to train its pilots and use Royal Canadian Air Force instructors instead. To be a flying instructor, the candidate had to be much better than an average pilot. The instructor had to know everything about planes and the science of flying. He also had to be very brave — imagine climbing into a cockpit of an aircraft with a nervous student about to take off and land for the first time. Many instructors risked their lives hundreds of times this way and many were killed or injured by their students.

Despite the high skill and courage necessary to qualify for their jobs, flying instructors were often looked down on by other airmen. Even the general population didn't give them proper credit because they didn't serve overseas. All the pilots who graduated from the BCATP owed their wings to the valiant instructors who trained them. All BCATP pilots who survived the war owed their lives to the skills their instructors taught them.

Many flight instructors repeatedly requested to be transferred overseas where they could prove themselves by flying combat missions. Most were turned down because they were considered too valuable. A combat flyer can take credit for every victory he or she achieves against an enemy, but a flying instructor has a claim on every victory of all the pilots he or she trained.

And yet, to this day, flying instructors who spent the Second World War risking their lives in Canada aren't considered "veterans" by the Canadian government. This unfortunate circumstance has more than just a social stigma. Former flight instructors don't qualify for as many government benefits as veterans, and it still irks them more than 60 years later to be treated as second-class military personnel by their own government despite their expertise and heroism.

4 Raising Cain in a Harvard

Charley and the other nine instructor candidates were sent to Trenton, Ontario, for further training. After being told what to do for so long, it was hard for many of them to adjust to being the person now giving orders. Several of the highest-scoring students were also promoted to pilot officer, the lowest commissioned rank in the RCAF and comparable to second lieutenant. Now, as he walked around Base Trenton, Charley was saluted by leading aircraftmen and even corporals and sergeants. It amazed Charley to think that exactly a year ago he had never even sat in an airplane. Now he was a full-fledged Harvard instructor!

With his instructor's course complete, Charley received orders to report back to Dunnville to teach on Harvards in October 1941. This seemingly innocent directive didn't go down well with his commander at Dunnville, however. Group Captain Allan Hall was very old school. He was so old school that his service number only had two digits (C-19) because he had joined the RCAF on the day it was created in 1924.

When he arrived in Dunnville, Charley was told to report to Hall. When Charley did, the group captain said, "Fox, I don't agree with this posting. You were here being taught by flight sergeants just six weeks ago. Do you think it's right that they'll now have to salute you on the base where everyone can see?"

"No, sir," Charley replied. He really didn't care about being saluted by anybody, but he knew the right answer was always to agree with your group captain.

Hall tried hard to have Charley posted to another base, but even possessing a two-digit service number had its limits. Charley stayed in Dunnville where, as it turned out, his former instructors didn't have a problem saluting him — or at least they never showed it.

Charley had other things on his mind, anyway. With his wings won and

> **FASCINATING FACT**
> **Royal Canadian Air Force Ranks**
>
> Like the other branches of the military, the Royal Canadian Air Force had a two-tier rank system of commissioned officers and enlisted men. In the Second World War most RCAF recruits started out as aircraftman two (acey ducey) and the promotions upward were leading aircraftman, corporal, sergeant, flight sergeant, warrant officer two, and finally warrant officer one. From bottom to top, the commissioned officers started as pilot officer, flying officer, flight lieutenant, squadron leader, wing commander, group captain, and upward to higher ranks. Because Charley Fox scored so high in his tests (89 percent was his final average), he was promoted from an enlisted man to a commissioned officer. Students who scored lower in their tests but still qualified for their wings became pilot sergeants.

no overseas posting likely for a while, he decided it was time to get married. He and Helen were wedded in early 1942, and their first home was in the married officers' quarters at Base Dunnville. Charley was pleased that Helen took to military life readily. All her life she had been a noted soprano in Guelph, and she and three other servicemen's wives formed a small choir for the base church.

Instructing was both satisfying and tragic for Charley. He loved to see nervous students bloom the minute they felt the wind under their wings. On the other hand, he occasionally had to dismiss completely hopeless candidates. Worse still, he sometimes lost students to accidents.

One cloudy day a student got lost trying to fly in formation. When they entered the clouds, the other airplanes became ghosts — mere dark shadows rising and falling with the turbulence and gusts of wind. The confused student nearly hit Charley four or five times inside the cloud, then panicked and pulled back on his controls too hard and went into a spin. Charley had three other students to worry about, so all he could do was continue flying and hope for the best. When they landed, they were saddened to hear that the student hadn't recovered from the spin and had crashed.

Department of National Defence PL-2079

Due to its high speed and responsive controls, the Harvard trainer was also known as the "Yellow Peril" because many students found it much more challenging to fly. Deaths in the pilot training program averaged five a week.

On another occasion Charley was able to salvage the career of an Australian student pilot who seemed perfectly fine in the air but always lost his nerve when he approached the runway. As he neared the ground, he'd begin to oversteer on the rudder, causing the tail to seesaw and nearly crashing the plane.

Most pilots had already checked out after eight hours. This poor young man was up to 16 and on the verge of being washed out, but Charley suddenly had an idea. The next time the student made a bad landing, instead of shouting at him like some of the other flying instructors did, Charley said, "You know, I think there's something wrong with your rear wheel." Charley had already told the lead mechanic to go over to the student's plane, inspect the wheel, and pronounce it broken no matter what shape it was in.

As expected, the Australian student made another perfectly terrible landing. Charley and the mechanic walked out to the Harvard with him, and the mechanic said, "No wonder you're having so much trouble." Then he proceeded to "fix" the perfectly good wheel by loosening and tightening a few bolts.

"Try it now," Charley said. The student took off, did a circuit, and came down for a perfect landing. He repeated this feat a half-dozen times and went on to earn his wings with the rest of his class.

Although Charley and his fellow instructors were now officers and in charge of teaching students to fly, it was also still a fact that most of them were young men barely out of their teens. When they were in front of students or their superior officers, Charley and the other instructors acted the way they were expected to — serious, stern, and safety-conscious. Whenever they got a chance to be by themselves, however, they often behaved like all young men with high-powered machines at their disposal.

On foggy days or when the clouds were low, Group Captain Hall declared "instructors' flying weather," meaning that only instructors could fly. In theory this gave instructors a chance to improve their skills. In practice it also provided them with opportunities to let off steam. On mist-shrouded days Charley and one or two of his fellow instructors would solemnly climb into their Harvards and take off into the overcast sky. Once out of sight of their superior officers and the public, the instructors found endless ways to amuse themselves.

Sometimes they played aerial tag, one Harvard diving and banking through the clouds while the others tried to stay on his tail. Other times they dropped to "the deck" to see how close to the ground they could get without crashing. They also played follow the leader as they popped over trees and passed under telephone wires at more than 160 kilometres per hour. Flying low to the ground was called "buzzing" because a plane's propeller nearly touched the grass like a lawnmower.

There was a prisoner of war camp for German soldiers near Port Colborne on Lake Erie where the inmates were required to dig peat, a mossy type of earth used like fire logs. Charley and his friends thought it was funny to sneak up on the working prisoners and buzz them as they dug in the peat bog, causing them to jump into the swampy trench face first. One German prisoner became so annoyed at being buzzed that he threw his shovel at the Harvards as they passed overhead. Surprisingly, the shovel actually jammed itself into the canvas-covered wing of one plane. The pilot heard a bang but didn't see the shovel stuck into the bottom of his wing. The foreign object didn't affect the plane while it was flying, but as the pilot attempted to land, the implement's long wooden handle caught the runway, ripped a big hole in the Harvard wing, and almost completely wrecked the plane. The pilot had a hard time explaining to Group Captain Hall how a shovel had become lodged in his wing. Fortunately, there was no other evidence to the contrary, so Hall grudgingly accepted the theory that perhaps someone had left a shovel on the runway. To this day, if he is still alive, there is a former German soldier who doesn't know he was probably the only person in the Second World War to down an enemy aircraft with a shovel.

Sometimes instructors took off for night-flying exercises. One instructor, Bob Black, liked to play practical jokes on railway engineers at night. When Black flew in the evening and spotted a freight train chugging along, he swept down and charged straight at the locomotive at track level. Then he switched on the Harvard's single landing headlight and made the engineer think another train was racing toward him. Showers of sparks flew as the engineer braked and the train came to a shrieking halt. The rest of the crew came running forward to find out what the problem was, but there was never anything to see because Black shut off his headlight and veered away at the last second as the screeching train brakes masked the roar of his retreat. The railway people always complained to the flight school, but because there were usually several pilots out practising night flying they were never able to prove who the trickster was.

Perhaps the most famous practical joke to come out of the Dunnville flight school occurred in plain sight of hundreds of construction workers at Niagara Falls. In 1938 an old steel bridge between Canada and the United States was wrecked by a jam of ice in the Niagara River. A new steel construction, the Peace Bridge, was erected with a big arch underneath to make sure the bridge wouldn't be vulnerable to future ice jams. The bridge was nearly completed in 1941, and the steel arch proved irresistible to Sergeant Cap Foster and Leading Aircraftman Bill Olmstead, the former an instructor, the latter a promising student.

Charley believed that Cap Foster was probably the best stunt pilot in the RCAF. In fact, the standing joke was that Cap's students spent more time flying upside down than right side up. During the Peace Bridge incident, Foster was in control as he and Olmstead raced down the Niagara Gorge, a place that was technically off limits. When Foster spotted the bridge directly in front, he decided not to pass just under the bridge but to loop it. Because the bridge was still under construction, safety nets still hung below it, forcing Foster to almost touch the water before he pulled back on the joystick and made the plane climb. He and Olmstead went straight up, then turned upside down and dived for the freezing water of the Niagara River. At the last moment they pulled up and passed under the bridge a second time. Then, with the throttle full out, they climbed into the clouds again.

Foster and Olmstead escaped being charged and possibly thrown out of pilots' school because witnesses could only identify two of the four small registration numbers painted on the wings and sides of the plane. An order came down to reduce registration numbers to two and to make them much larger. "That kind of spoiled the fun," Charley later said.

Occasionally, flying instructors played hooky and landed somewhere to enjoy a steaming cup of coffee at a civilian restaurant. Once, while winter-flying near Galt (now part of Cambridge), Ontario, Charley and another instructor glanced down and spied a yellow Harvard sitting on the ice of Puslinch Lake. Harvards weren't equipped with radios, so Charley signalled that he was descending to see if the pilot was in trouble. Charley noticed that the engine of the plane on the ice was still running, but the pilot was waving at him to come on down. He had never made a landing on a frozen lake before but figured if the man below could do it, so could he. First Charley and then the other instructor landed and taxied up to the parked Harvard.

When they asked what the stranger's problem was, he replied, "No problem. Come in for a coffee."

Sure enough, there was a restaurant called the Wastika Inn on the shore. Hot coffee after a cold trip in a Harvard sounded good, so they went inside where the owners made a big fuss over the visiting pilots and insisted they sit in huge wicker chairs that looked like thrones. The owners said they were going to crown Charley "King of Puslinch Lake" and gave him a cup of coffee. But the chair was wired so that he and his wingman got a shot of electricity in their bums as soon as the coffee touched their lips. They jumped into the air and ended up covered in coffee. "There, you're both Kings of Puslinch Lake," the innkeeper said, laughing.

The only person who had managed to top Charley in the pilot course was F. Layton Exel, a born mathematician. One evening Exel mathematically calculated that a Harvard didn't need ice to land on a lake. By his computations he figured that if a Harvard was going fast enough and a lake was completely calm, the plane could actually water-ski across the lake with its landing gear down. None of the other instructors believed him, so on a rare day when Lake Erie was as smooth as glass he decided to put his theory to the test. While Charley and the other pilots watched from above, he lowered his landing gear and carefully descended until his wheels touched the water. At the very least Charley expected the plane to flip and

Exel to get a very wet landing. To their amazement, though, the math whiz was right and his Harvard slid across Lake Erie like a champion water skier until he pushed the throttle forward and took off again. After the war, Charley found a photograph of some South African pilots doing the same thing with their Harvards. The way stories travel in the military, perhaps they had heard about Exel's experiment on Lake Erie in 1943.

In 1941 Charley and another flying buddy nearly got arrested for an illegal cup of coffee on the wrong side of the border. On a flying instructors' weather day they flew south in heavy fog and accidentally crossed over Lake Erie into New York State. It was a long way back, so while they were there they decided to land in Jamestown, New York, and grab a cup of "joe" for the return trip. The United States was still neutral then and any foreign servicemen, Canadian or German, who entered American territory were supposed to be arrested and jailed for the duration of the war. Charley and his companion were just finishing their coffee when someone in the control tower phoned down to say that the sheriff was coming to arrest them. Fortunately, Charley and the other pilot had left the engines running in their Harvards and were able to jump into their planes and race down the runway before the sheriff could catch up with them.

But flying school had a deadly side that could appear at any time. One day flying instructors Norman Kirk and Tom MacIntyre took off together in a Harvard for some routine practice. No one ever knew exactly what happened, but the Harvard went into a steep climb right after takeoff, then stalled and crashed into the nearby Grand River. Both pilots were killed instantly.

Because Charley, at 21, was slightly older than the rest of his colleagues, Group Captain Hall assigned him the duty of investigating officer. The bodies had been retrieved from the wreckage and were being kept in the morgue of the local funeral home. Charley contacted the undertaker and arranged to stop by the funeral home to identify the bodies and retrieve any personal effects that could be sent to the victims' families.

Since there was no doubt about the identity of the dead men, the funeral director suggested that Charley needn't bother to see the battered bodies of his two friends because it would likely upset him. But an investigating officer was supposed to identify the bodies of downed flyers no matter how upsetting the ordeal was. Charley thought immediately about what his father would do, and he knew that his dad would say that if a person was given a job to do, he had to see it through to the end. When Charley told the funeral director he had to identify the bodies officially, the man nodded and said, "Okay, but I'll be right behind you."

As soon as Charley stepped into the morgue, the combined odour of gasoline, oil, river water, and death hit him hard. His two friends were lying on cots in front of him. Just as the undertaker had said, they were badly disfigured. In a last tribute to Kirk and MacIntyre, Charley forced himself to remove their rings, watches, and wallets so that their families would have something to remember them by.

Charley greatly enjoyed his days as a flying instructor, but he still routinely submitted requests to be posted overseas. He continued applying for combat duty even after he received the disturbing news that both Wally Floody and Larry Summers had been shot down over German-occupied France.

FASCINATING FACT
Walter Floody — Tunneller from Timmins

Before joining the Royal Canadian Air Force, Walter "Wally" Floody worked as a "mucker" deep underground in the gold mines of Timmins, Ontario. Wally's job was to move tonnes of rocks and sludge from the mine tunnels up to the surface. When Wally moved on from Dunnville, he was trained to fly Spitfires and then posted to RCAF Squadron 401 stationed at Biggin Hill, England. His flying career was short-lived, though. He was shot down on his first combat mission over France and was captured by the Germans on October 28, 1941. After numerous escape attempts, Floody was sent to Stalag Luft III, a brand-new "escape-proof" camp run by the Luftwaffe in Poland. Because of Wally's pre-war mining experience, he was quickly recruited by the POWs' Escape Committee, which was determined to pull off the largest mass breakout in history. Wally's knowledge of tunnel construction proved invaluable as he not only devised ways to move hundreds of tonnes of sand from the escape tunnels but also disposed of the "spoil," the tunnel sand that didn't match the earth on top of the ground. Wally was supposed to be one of the hundred-plus prisoners chosen to take part in the escape, but he was suddenly transferred to another camp weeks before the breakout took place. The transfer likely saved his life. On the night of the escape, 76 prisoners made it out of the camp. Three achieved freedom, but 50 of the remaining 73 prisoners were shot on Adolf Hitler's personal orders. For his sacrifice and hard work at Stalag III, Wally received the Order of the British Empire from King George VI. A book and a movie called *The Great Escape* were based on the events at Stalag III. Wally Floody was a technical adviser for the movie, and the character played by Charles Bronson in the film is based on him.

In 1943 Charley's wish was finally granted. He found out the news shortly after Helen told him she was pregnant. They were still newlyweds, but now he was about to go overseas and risk his life in a war. He wouldn't see his new son until 1945 when he returned to Canada from Germany.

5 Combat Training

Although Charley hadn't been pleased when he was told to report to instructor duties instead of accompanying his class to fighter training school, he later decided that the posting probably saved his life. Unlike most of his classmates who only had 50 hours or more flight time in an advanced trainer like the Harvard, Charley had more than 1,500, so flying was as natural to him as walking or breathing. He had practised numerous aerobatic manoeuvres so many times that he could fly sideways, upside down, and sometimes almost backward as he tipped up into a steep climb, stalled, then recovered from the stall.

In May 1943, Charley was transferred to Bagotville, an RCAF base 160 kilometres due north of Quebec City. Here Harvards and Hurricane fighter pilots trained side by side. A squadron of Hurricanes was also based at Bagotville to protect the nearby Alcan aluminum plant, which was turning out much-needed *matériel* for the war. There were also long-range patrol aircraft stationed in Bagotville, which flew over the Gulf of St. Lawrence hunting for the German submarines that were sinking Allied ships as they attempted to move men and supplies to Britain. That meant the Bagotville airfield and the skies overhead were always crowded with various types of aircraft flying at different altitudes and speeds.

Charley's first fighter training was in Hurricanes. Although by 1943 Hurricanes were considered almost obsolete, they had twice the speed and twice the rate of climb of the Harvards

Charley was used to. Despite the raw power provided by the Hurricane's 12-cylinder, 1,200-horsepower Rolls-Royce engine, Charley found the plane to be a very stable aircraft with no bad habits. Although Spitfires would later become the "love" of his life, Charley greatly respected the Hurricane and understood why the Luftwaffe failed to win the Battle of Britain when faced with determined pilots in such planes.

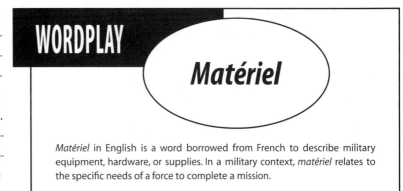

WORDPLAY

Matériel

Matériel in English is a word borrowed from French to describe military equipment, hardware, or supplies. In a military context, *matériel* relates to the specific needs of a force to complete a mission.

On June 1, 1943, Charley was practising formation flying and was leading two other Harvards back to base at 900 metres when, above them, a flight of three Hurricanes approached at about 1,500 metres. The Hurricane pilots sometimes used other Allied aircraft as practice targets if they happened to see them in the air, but Harvards and Hurricanes weren't supposed to mix because the vastly different speed capabilities of each aircraft could result in a crash. With that in mind Charley was surprised to observe the Hurricane leader dip his wings, a signal to his mates that he was going to attempt a mock attack. The Hurricane dived from behind in the classic dogfighting tactic of trying to sneak up from behind and below.

To show the Hurricane pilot he had been spotted and therefore his attack was foiled, Charley ordered the flight of Harvards to break right, which meant they all immediately turned right to dodge the much faster Hurricane. Tragically, the young fighter pilot misjudged his G-forces as he pulled out of the dive. He likely passed out and hurtled at the three slower-moving Harvards like a blind missile. Having lost sight of the Hurricane, Charley thought all was well until something smashed up through the front of his Harvard and tore away his engine and propeller.

Charley was knocked unconscious by the collision. When he came to, he groggily grabbed the controls and tried to fly. Through blood-smeared eyes he noticed he no longer

FASCINATING FACT
Hawker Hurricane — Workhorse of the Royal Air Force

The Hurricane was the aircraft that replaced the Hawker Hart as the British Commonwealth's primary fighter plane. Both were built by Hawker Aircraft Limited, the same company responsible for creating many of Britain's warplanes. Trying to save money and speed up production, the designers of the Hurricane used parts and designs from their earlier lines of biplanes, so the Hurricane was still partially constructed of wood and fabric like the fighters of the First World War. This turned out to be an advantage when Hurricane pilots came up against the devastating power of the Messerschmitt's cannons — the wood-and-canvas fuselage and tail could endure the explosive shells better than the all-metal frame of the more modern Spitfire. Damaged Hurricanes were also more easily repaired by ground crews.

More than 500 Hurricanes were in service at the beginning of the Second World War, and they provided the backbone of the United Kingdom's air defences during the Battle of Britain. Because it was such a beautiful aircraft, the Spitfire received more public attention than the slightly hunch-backed Hurricane, but of the 2,739 German airplanes shot down in the Battle of Britain, the dowdy Hurricane accounted for 1,593 of them. This feat was partly due to the fact that Hurricanes still outnumbered Spitfires by a large majority and also because the Hurricane was a very stable plane to fly, which enabled pilots to fire their guns with extreme accuracy. The Hurricane served in all theatres of the war, including France, North Africa, Norway, and the Far East. Three thousand Hurricanes even served on the Russian front.

Like the Spitfire, the Hurricane was initially armed with eight .303 machine guns. Later variants carried 12 .303 machine guns, some carried four 20 mm cannons, and one version boasted two 40 mm automatic cannons. A light bomber version, known as the Hurribomber, was produced by converting the fighter to carry two bombs weighing up to 226 kilograms each under its wings.

Almost 15,000 Hurricanes were built before they were finally phased out of production in 1944. Fourteen hundred Hurricanes were manufactured at the Canada Car & Foundry in Fort William (now part of Thunder Bay), Ontario. After the war, surplus Hurricanes were bought by air forces around the world, and some remained in service until the mid-1950s.

had an engine or a propeller. The Harvard was gliding, but not too well. When he glanced left, he saw that the Hurricane's left wing had also sheared off the Harvard's left tailplane and left wing. The Harvard was slowly spinning toward the ground, now about 600 metres away. Still barely conscious, Charley let his hours of drill take over. He unhooked his safety harness, slid the canopy back, climbed out onto the right wing, and dived away from the plane to avoid being hit by the tail.

In seconds Charley was plummeting toward the ground at more than 160 kilometres per hour. With his right hand he groped for the D-ring connected to the rip cord to open his parachute, but his right arm wasn't working well. As he fumbled with the ring, he thought his uniform was slippery with grease. With the ground rushing up he said to himself, "Fox, you're going to make a big splat if you don't get that D-ring pulled." Finally, with his left hand, he found and pulled the ring and the chute opened above him with a loud snap.

Charley was barely awake enough to notice he was drifting backward and heading for a forest full of pine trees. His first thought was "Ouch! They're pointy!" Then he crossed his feet and pulled his arms in tight, knowing that a sharp tree branch could puncture a lung or slice open an artery. At the last moment, when he realized he was about to smash against a huge rock, he pulled on his parachute risers. This action caused him to miss the rock, but he still crashed hard into some trees.

For a second time Charley was knocked cold. When he woke up, he was blind in his right eye, his right arm felt broken, and most of his right side was numb. As his left eye focused, he saw that what he had thought was engine grease on his uniform was actually his own blood freely flowing from a head wound. Despite his wounds, Charley unhooked his harness and dragged his parachute open so that it would be

WORDPLAY

Cockpits and Dogfights

As early as the First World War, fighter pilots developed their own unique jargon for parts of the airplane and tactics. Two such terms are *cockpit* and *dogfight*. A cockpit is the small, confined place where a plane's pilot sits. This word was borrowed from the Royal Navy, which used it to describe a small, box-like place in a ship's deck where crew members sat to protect themselves against high seas and bad weather. *Cockpit*, in turn, was taken from the ancient brutal practice of cockfighting in which two grown roosters are thrown into a ring to fight until one kills the other. This "sport" was popular in Britain until it was banned in 1849, but it is still practised in some parts of the world today. Even in contemporary North America and Europe, cockfighting still flourishes clandestinely and illegally. A dogfight is an aerial combat between two or more fighter planes. The term derives from observing how dogs actually fight. In most conflicts between dogs each canine typically tries to get above and behind its opponent so it can bite without being bitten back. This tactic was favoured by fighter pilots because if they got behind their opponents they could shoot at them, but their adversaries couldn't fire back. Some air forces attempted to remedy this problem by installing rear gunners on fighter planes, but that proved unsatisfactory. The Messerschmitt Bf 110 was a typical example. The German plane was easy prey for Spitfires and even Hurricanes because the British flyers only had to cruise a little lower than the Bf 110, making it difficult for the rear gunner to shoot at his target without destroying his own aircraft's tail. Even if he did get off a decent shot, the rear gunner was outgunned eight to one by larger-calibre weapons. The added weight of the extra airman and his gun station also made the Bf 110 slower and less manoeuvrable. Furthermore, when a Bf 110 was shot down, Germany lost two airmen instead of one. In the Battle of Britain the Bf 110 had the dubious distinction of being the only "fighter" that needed an escort of other fighters.

Library and Archives Canada PA-037482

In June 1940 in France, Royal Air Force pilots of 87 Squadron scramble to reach their Hurricanes to oppose incoming Luftwaffe fighters. Many non-British pilots served in RAF squadrons before all-Canadian, American, Polish, Czechoslovak, Australian, South African, and New Zealander units were formed.

visible from the air. Without radios the Harvards couldn't contact Bagotville to report the accident, so one of the planes circled over Charley's position while the other flew back to base to get help.

Eventually, two French-Canadian farmers found Charley in the forest and helped him limp about a kilometre out of the bush to their farmhouse. The wife of one of the farmers heated up some water on the wood stove and poured it into a bowl for Charley to wash the blood off his face. With a warm, wet cloth Charley carefully bathed his right eye and was relieved to discover he wasn't blind. He was fascinated by the fact that he could glimpse his skull through the cut on his forehead, and ran his finger along it to make sure it wasn't cracked or splintered. Not surprisingly, Charley began to feel dizzy, and his kind hosts helped him to a cot until some RCAF personnel arrived and took him back to Bagotville.

At the base it turned out that Charley's arm wasn't broken, merely badly bruised from being knocked against the right side of the Harvard's cockpit when the Hurricane hit on the left. When the doctor prepared to sew up the gash on Charley's head, a junior medical officer pleaded with the senior officer to be allowed to sew up the wound, claiming he needed the practice. The doctor said okay, so on top of his injuries, Charley got to be a practice sewing dummy. Charley spent four days in the hospital and then was given a 10-day leave. He was back in the cockpit flying by June 20.

FASCINATING FACT
Hitting the Silk

Parachutes have been around for centuries. Some historians claim that a Muslim scientist named Abbas Ibn Firnas leaped from the top of a mosque's minaret in Córdoba, Spain, in the ninth century wearing a parachute-like cloak and survived with just a few bruises. Leonardo da Vinci designed a parachute in 1483 but never tested it. Scientists in 2006 actually built da Vinci's device and proved that it worked. Unfortunately, da Vinci's chute weighed 85 kilograms because the twenty-first-century scientists employed materials that were available only in late-fifteenth-century Italy. Various working parachute designs were developed in the late nineteenth and early twentieth centuries, but all were too large, too heavy, too complicated, or too unreliable to use as battle equipment.

During the First World War, thousands of airplane pilots and crew members were killed on both sides because there still was no compact and reliable parachute available for flyers to wear. Allied generals resisted giving their airmen parachutes because they thought their pilots would jump to safety rather than fight. Fortunately for German pilots, their commanders had a better opinion of them and by 1918 parachutes were issued to all flyers. Tragically, many parachutes failed and the airmen died, anyway.

In 1919 Leslie Irwin, an American stuntman, borrowed a sewing machine and created a small, lightweight parachute that could easily fit inside an airplane cockpit. He tested his chute himself, and other than suffering a broken ankle from a clumsy landing (there were no parachute schools yet), he considered the test a complete success. Both the American Army Air Corps and the Royal Air Force agreed and made the Irwin chute standard equipment for their crews.

Irwin had so many orders that he opened factories in the United States and Britain. In 1922 he wisely took the advice of two journalists who suggested he form a club whose members were people who had been saved by an Irwin parachute. Irwin issued a press statement, promising to give a gold pin and a certificate to anyone who could prove that his or her life had been saved by an Irwin-style chute. The inventor named his brainstorm the Caterpillar Club because the canopies of his chutes were made of silk, a lightweight but very strong cloth made from threads spun by silkworms, a type of caterpillar that turns into a moth.

Ironically, the Caterpillar Club is probably the only organization in the world where the members can't join voluntarily. They must face near-certain death in a disabled aircraft and have escape by parachute as their only way to survive. By the end of the Second World War, more than 35,000 people, most of them Allied flyers, were official members of the club. It is estimated that more than 100,000 people owe their lives to Irwin-style parachutes, including former U.S. President George H.W. Bush, astronaut John Glenn, and aviation hero Charles Lindbergh. And Charley Fox.

There was an official hearing to determine the cause of the mid-air collision, and Charley was cleared of any blame for the crash. Unfortunately, the Hurricane pilot had died, but it was impossible to tell whether he was killed in the initial collision or if he died as his plane spun to the ground and exploded into flames. Charley felt sorry for the pilot but knew that all kinds of bad things happened during war. Not only had Charley survived a deadly crash, but he was now officially a member of the Caterpillar Club (see "Hitting the Silk").

6 Over There

Charley completed his fighter training in early August 1943 and was told he would be shipping to Europe later that month. He said goodbye to the still-pregnant Helen, and she returned to her family in Guelph. Charley then took a train to Halifax to catch a ride across the Atlantic Ocean in the *Queen Mary*, a civilian liner that had been converted into a "super trooper" capable of transporting a small army in a single trip.

It seemed like "standing room only" as Charley went up the gangplank. He spotted sailors and servicemen everywhere. There were soldiers crowded on the decks and crammed into every passageway. Because Charley was an officer, he was billeted in a first-class cabin with a fancy marble-tiled floor and bird's-eye maple wall panelling. Unfortunately, he had to share the cabin with eight other officers. The room had three three-tier bunks crammed into it, but at least they had their own washroom.

From Halifax the *Queen Mary*'s powerful engines enabled the ship to cross the Atlantic in just four and a half days. Charley landed in Scotland and was then sent by train to England. He was told to stop at the RCAF depot in a town called Bournemouth and wait for orders about where to report. Three days after he arrived he noticed a soldier with a shoulder patch that said 12th Field Regiment. He knew that his brother, Ted, was with that unit, so he asked the soldier if his battery was the 16th 43rd. The soldier said it was.

FASCINATING FACT
Queen Mary Goes to War

Before the development of passenger airplanes, people crossed oceans on massive ships called ocean liners. One of the largest, fastest, and most luxurious of these vessels was the Royal Mail Ship (RMS) *Queen Mary*. The *Queen Mary* started regular passenger service in 1936. At 310 metres long it was 42 metres longer than the *Titanic* and could travel at just over 30 nautical miles per hour, making it one of the fastest ships in the world. During peacetime, the *Queen Mary* normally carried 2,139 passengers. After the Second World War commenced in 1939, the ship was stripped of all its fine furniture and jammed with bunks to accommodate more than 16,000 soldiers per trip. Decked out in wartime grey paint, the *Queen Mary* and its younger sister ship, RMS *Queen Elizabeth*, were nicknamed the Grey Ghosts because of their ability to disappear over the horizon at high speed. The *Queen Mary* and *Queen Elizabeth* even had some claws for scrapping; both were fitted with 20 mm Oerlikon cannons to deter enemy dive bombers and submarines.

The Germans knew what a valuable contribution the *Queen Mary* and *Queen Elizabeth* were making to the Allied war effort, so Adolf Hitler personally promised an Iron Cross with an Oak Leaf Cluster and the equivalent of a quarter-million dollars to any U-boat captain who could sink either one of them. Because of the liners' superior speed, though, no one ever collected the prize.

Not just ordinary soldiers trusted the *Queen Mary* with their safety. British Prime Minister Winston Churchill made three round trips across the Atlantic to meet with U.S. President Franklin D. Roosevelt and Canadian Prime Minister William Lyon Mackenzie King.

In October 1942 the *Queen Mary* collided with the HMS *Curacoa*, a slower-moving escort cruiser. The Royal Navy vessel sank almost instantly, resulting in the deaths of 338 British sailors. After that tragic accident, it was decided that the *Queen Mary* and *Queen Elizabeth* would travel without escort, and the two liners served the remainder of the war sailing solo around the world.

Between them, the *Queen Mary* and *Queen Elizabeth* ferried more than 1.5 million soldiers across the Atlantic and Pacific Oceans and journeyed nearly 2 million kilometres. By moving so many soldiers so far so fast, Churchill later said that the two ships shortened the war by a year. After the war, the *Queen Mary* and *Queen Elizabeth* were returned to their original splendour and dominated the tourist travel market until long-distance passenger jets made them obsolete in the 1960s. The *Queen Mary* is now a tourist attraction and luxury hotel in Long Beach, California.

After asking around, Charley found Ted, and the Fox brothers had a satisfying reunion. It had been only 26 months since they had lived under the same roof in Arkell, but it seemed as if a hundred years had passed. Now, thousands of kilometres from home and about to go to war, they realized how much they meant to each other.

It took a very trivial incident, though, to make Charley realize he was finally in the war. When he returned to the RAF station in Bournemouth, he went to eat in the mess and was served a plate of food. After he finished his meal, he was still hungry, so he went back for seconds. "Sorry, sir," the orderly said. "There's a war on. There are no seconds." Even though there was rationing in Canada, there had never been a time when there were no seconds. In

Britain, however, people had been living without seconds for more than three years.

While he was waiting in Bournemouth, Charley ran into a few other familiar faces. Andy Howden, Howie Steen, and Sandy Borland were schoolmates of Charley's who had joined the RCAF after he had. They were all on the verge of being shipped to their squadrons across Britain, but they had time to pose for a quick picture that they called "Four Guys from Guelph." Of those four, two would be dead within a year.

From Bournemouth, Charley was sent to Number 57 Operational Training Unit (OTU) in Eshott in northern England, where he trained on Spitfires. From the moment his Spitfire's

FASCINATING FACT
Supermarine Spitfire —
Trophy Hunter to Hun Hunter

The Spitfire is possibly the most famous fighter airplane of all time. Lovely to look at yet deadly in combat, it arrived on the scene just as Britain stood alone against the mighty German Luftwaffe. The Spitfire is a true Thoroughbred. Its airframe is descended from a series of trophy-winning racing planes, and its supercharged 12-cylinder Rolls-Royce engine evolved from British race cars.

The Spitfire was the creation of Reginald Mitchell, an engineer who designed racing seaplanes for a company called Supermarine. From above the Spitfire's wings resemble a surfboard — wide in the middle and pointed at each end. The reason for this was that the British needed a wing wide enough to hold eight machine guns and yet remain aerodynamic. This famous elliptical wing gives the Spitfire an unmistakable outline.

The Luftwaffe countered the Spitfire with improved versions of the Messerschmitt Bf 109 and new fighters like the Focke-Wulf Fw 190, which sometimes gave the advantage to the Germans. Fortunately, each time the Nazis came up with something new, the British were able to improve the Spitfire so that it matched or exceeded the abilities of its opponents. More than 22,500 Spitfires were produced, and it was the only fighter that entered service at the beginning of Second World War that was still being manufactured several years after. The Spitfire began the war with a maximum airspeed of 540 kilometres per hour and was armed with eight .303 machine guns. It was eventually upgraded so that it could fly at just over 640 kilometres per hour, and later Spitfires were armed with up to four automatic 20 mm cannons. The Royal Navy had a seagoing version of the Spitfire known as the Seafire. The major difference was that the Seafire had collapsible wings so that more of them could be stored aboard aircraft carriers. Two dozen variants of the Spitfire were produced. The last version was a much faster, deadlier, and more powerful plane. However, it was also uglier, since to increase roll speed the beautiful elliptical point wings were sheared flat.

Mitchell originally wanted to christen his craft "The Shrew," after a small but pugnacious carnivorous mouse-like creature. But Sir Robert MacLean, director of the factory manufacturing the plane, changed the name to Spitfire because the new fighter reminded him of his little daughter. Spitfire is an old English word for a feisty female who won't back down from a fight. The airplane's creator wasn't impressed with the name change and is said to have grumbled, "That's just the sort of silly name they'd think of."

wheels left the ground, Charley knew he had found the love of his life — at least in airplanes. In his hands, he often said, the Spitfire didn't just fly; it danced through the sky like "the loveliest lady in the ballroom." Charley knew the Spitfire was faster than even the Hurricane and that it could outperform any other plane on a climbing turn, which was the Spitfire pilot's surefire escape route in a dogfight.

Training on Spitfires until the end of December, Charley then returned to Bournemouth for reassignment. For six weeks he practised firing his guns at targets towed by obsolete bombers, or he dropped smoke bombs on ground targets to simulate the real bombs he would drop someday.

When he checked out on Spitfires and fighter school, Charley was transferred to 412 Squadron, which was stationed at Biggin Hill, one of the RAF's largest and oldest air bases. Biggin had been one of the very first airports built in Britain when it became the main base of

FASCINATING FACT
Sonnet to the Spitfire

Charley Fox wasn't the only pilot to fall in love with the Spitfire. John Gillespie Magee, Jr., was an Anglo-American teenager who won a scholarship to Yale University, but when the Second World War broke out, he put his studies on hold and travelled to Canada to join the Royal Canadian Air Force. He graduated from pilot school and was stationed in England. In September 1941 he was given the latest model of Spitfire to test, and as the beautiful fighter rose majestically to more than 10,000 metres, certain words resonated in Magee's mind. The words kept coming back to him, so he jotted them down as a sonnet as soon as he landed. Later he sent the poem to his mother in the United States. Magee called the poem "High Flight," and it describes the sensation of flying a Spitfire.

Oh! I have slipped the surly bonds of Earth
And danced the skies on laughter-silvered wings;
Sunward I've climbed, and joined the tumbling mirth
Of sun-split clouds — and done a hundred things
You have not dreamed of — wheeled and soared and swung
High in the sunlit silence. Hov'ring there,
I've chased the shouting wind along, and flung
My eager craft through footless halls of air …
Up, up the long, delirious, burning blue
I've topped the wind-swept heights with easy grace
Where never lark, or ever eagle flew —
And, while with silent, lifting mind I've trod
The high untrespassed sanctity of space,
Put out my hand, and touched the face of God.

In December 1941, just three months after writing the sonnet, Magee was descending through a cloud over his air base in England when he collided with an Oxford bomber training aircraft that was taking off. Magee survived the crash but couldn't get his canopy open in time. He finally bailed out but was too low to the ground for his parachute to open. At the age of 19 he was dead. "High Flight" is the official poem of the RCAF and the Royal Air Force, and pilot cadets in the U.S. Air Force are required to memorize it as part of their training.

Department of National Defence PL-28263

Flight Lieutenant Charley Fox checks on his Spitfire's cannons in March 1944 in England before he takes off on a combat mission over France.

operations for the RAF during the First World War. The base was constructed on a hill overlooking London, which lay to the south. It started off as an early radio site, but the fledgling RAF was soon using the installation to defend London from Zeppelin and Gotha bomber raids, since the location gave British fighters a head start in altitude.

In the Second World War, Biggin Hill was again the centre of command during the Battle of Britain, with both Hurricane and Spitfire squadrons operating from there as Hermann Göring's Luftwaffe attacked both it and London. By the time Charley arrived, British, Polish, Dutch, Canadian, and American squadrons were crowding the runways, taking off, and returning from night and day raids in France and Holland.

Next to the other newly minted combat pilots, Charley felt slightly out of place as a "sprog," or new guy. Most of his fellow pilots were teenagers who had barely tasted their first beer or even asked a girl for a dance. Charley was 24, married, had a son, and was a flight lieutenant with more than 1,500 hours of flying experience. Sprogs were generally treated with gentle contempt the way any "new guy" on a team or in a class was. They weren't expected to have an opinion about anything because they hadn't seen the enemy yet. Sprogs weren't even allowed to have their own aircraft but had to "borrow" them from more experienced pilots. Charley was assigned VZ-D, a Spitfire belonging to fellow pilot "Junior" Bliss.

More than any other sprog, Charley was keenly aware that he had to prove himself to his squadron. He had already heard jokes being made, not about him but other "instructors" who were still "hiding" back in Canada. Charley was determined to demonstrate he was as good as anyone in the squadron as soon as he was given a chance.

So when Charley learned that his flight leader in 412 Squadron would be George Beurling, Canada's top ace and one of the highest-scoring fighter pilots in the British Empire, he was delighted. Beurling was one of the best pilots on either side in the war, and Charley knew it was a stroke of great fortune to make his first combat patrol under the ace's supervision. However, Charley's initial combat flight almost ended before it got off the ground.

The Germans flew in *Schwarm* or "Finger Four" formations. Partly because the Messerschmitt Bf 109 crashed so often on takeoff and landing, the Germans usually took off in well-spaced pairs so that if someone had an accident he wouldn't cause a pileup on the runway. They also flew in pairs while in the air so that each pilot could concentrate on the whole sky and look behind his partner to see if an Allied pilot was attempting to sneak up for an ambush. When attacking, the Germans broke off in pairs, called a *Rotte*, with the wingman covering the leader's blind spot during the attack. The leader of the formation was called a *Rottenführer*.

In the early days of the war Buzz Beurling was a vocal critic of the British "mother hen"

FASCINATING FACT
412 — Falcon Squadron

When the Royal Canadian Air Force's 412 Squadron was formed in June 1941, its pilots were given Spitfires, the British Commonwealth's best fighter plane. Within two months, 412 was flying missions over France and the Low Countries and went on to participate in major air battles to support Allied ground forces at Dieppe and during D-Day. Later the unit was involved in Operations Market Garden and Baseplate and saw action in the Battle of the Bulge. Besides fighting enemy aircraft, the 412 also performed ground-attack and dive-bombing operations, tasks the Spitfire hadn't originally been designed to do. Still, the 412 is credited with 106 destroyed enemy aircraft, 11 probables, and 46 damaged. The squadron also destroyed 250 enemy ground vehicles and 20 locomotives.

Many famous pilots served with the 412, including George "Buzz" Beurling (Canada's top ace), John Magee (author of the poem "High Flight"), and Arthur Bishop (son of Billy Bishop, Canada's top First World War ace). Twenty-five 412 pilots died in combat operations.

When the squadron was transferred to the French side of the English Channel, the ground crew had to take a crash course in infantry tactics because they were stationed so close to the front that there was a good chance their airfields could be attacked by the German army. Enemy snipers were still firing on the RCAF airstrip at Bény-sur-Mer in Normandy when the first 412 Spitfires arrived in France to drop off cold beer stored in their wing tanks.

The 412 was known as the Falcon Squadron, and its motto is *Promptus ad Vindictum* ("Swift to Avenge"). The squadron served as part of the Allied Occupation Force in Germany until it was disbanded in 1946. The unit, reformed as a transport squadron during the Cold War, is still in service today and is based in Ottawa.

In March 1944 in England, 412 Squadron Spitfires taxi out to the runway. Because most Second World War planes were "tail draggers," pilots couldn't see directly in front of their aircraft until they took off, so a ground crewman sat on one of the wings and guided his pilot to takeoff position.

formation, but all he received in response was a reputation as a troublemaker. He was later proved right when the Allied command adopted the German Finger Four after the Polish RAF squadrons, which also flew in *Schwarm* formations, performed better in combat than most other RAF squadrons.

It was standard British Commonwealth practice to have a whole flight of fighters take off at the same time in a tight formation. The idea was that the flight leader, who was the most experienced pilot, could better supervise the rest of his men the same way a mother hen took care of her chicks by covering them with her wing. However, taking off in a tightly packed formation was difficult and dangerous. On takeoff only the lead pilot actually watched where the flight was going, while each of the "chicks" had to focus on the airplane in front to avoid a collision.

There were also drawbacks to flying this way during patrol because once again only the leader had a clear field of vision while the other pilots struggled to stay in formation without crashing. The last plane was called "Tail-End Charlie" and was frequently in the most dangerous position, since it was often picked off by Axis pilots coming up from behind.

On this particular morning Buzz Beurling's pilots were taking off in a right-echelon formation. From above this formation resembled a flight of stairs, with Beurling as the top step on the left and the last step being Charley on the bottom right. Their mission was to take off and cross the English Channel, hook up with a flight of American Boston medium

WORDPLAY

Air Force Slang

All branches of the military have a rich abundance of slang. Here are some of the many terms that were common in the Royal Air Force and the Royal Canadian Air Force during the Second World War.

Ace — A pilot who has shot down five or more enemy airplanes.

Archie — Anti-aircraft fire.

Banana Boat — Aircraft carrier.

Bandits — Enemy aircraft.

Beehive — A tight formation of enemy bombers and fighters.

Blockbuster — A huge bomb.

Boomerang — A return to base before a mission is completed because of a technical problem with an aircraft.

Brass — High-ranking officers who have gold braid on their hats.

Bumf — Toilet paper, but also refers to unnecessary paperwork.

Caterpillar Club — Someone who has used a parachute to save his or her life (because parachutes were made from material spun by silkworms).

Crabbing Along — To fly at low altitude.

Cricket — German night fighter.

Deck — Ground or surface of a large body of water.

Ditch — Deliberately land in a large body of water to avoid crashing on land.

Flak — An acronym taken from the German Fl*iegerabwehrkanonen* from (*Flieger* or "flyer" plus *Abwehr* or "defence" plus *Kanonen* or "cannons").

Flamer — An aircraft that goes down in flames.

Flaming Onion — Anti-aircraft fire whose tracers seem to join together like a string of onions.

Gremlin — A mythical creature that is supposed to sabotage aircraft or cause unexplainable malfunctions.

Hedgehop — To fly so low that the aircraft skims the tops of trees and houses.

In the Drink — A crash landing in the water.

Mae West — An inflatable life vest that, when activated, made the wearer resemble the famous buxom American actress of the 1930s and 1940s.

Mahogany Spitfire — The "fighter" of someone who fights the war behind a desk.

Mess — The place where military personnel eat or drink.

Office — Cockpit.

Penguin — A new officer with no experience. He has wings but can't fly.

Play Pussy — To hide in the clouds like a cat stalking prey.

Port — The left side of an aircraft from the pilot's point of view.

Prang — To crash or to hit a target exactly.

Pulpit — Another term for the cockpit.

Rhubarb — To fly very low to the ground on a cloudy day while attacking enemy targets.

Scrub — To cancel a mission.

Sparks — The person responsible for the radio.

Sprog — A new recruit.

Starboard — The right side of an aircraft from the pilot's point of view.

Stooge — Second-in-command.

Tail-End Charlie — The last airplane in a formation and not a good place to be, since it was usually the first to be attacked.

Touch Bottom — To crash.

Waffle — To fly indecisively, or to lose control.

Wash Out — To fail.

Yellow Doughnut — An inflatable raft.

Yellow Peril — A training aircraft, especially a Harvard.

FASCINATING FACT
Buzz Beurling — Canada's Dark Ace

In the Second World War few pilots caused more controversy than Canadian ace George "Buzz" Beurling. Early in his life Beurling decided to be a pilot. He started flying lessons at the age of 14 and made his first solo flight two years later. While still a teenager he tried to join the Chinese air force, which was recruiting American pilots to fight the Japanese. But he had entered the United States illegally and was deported to Canada. He also volunteered to fly for the Finnish air force to fight the Soviets but was still under 21, so his father refused to sign the permission forms.

When the war began, Beurling attempted to join the Royal Canadian Air Force but was turned down because he didn't have a high-school diploma. He worked his way to Britain as a deckhand on a ship loaded with explosives, applied to the Royal Air Force, and was rejected because he hadn't brought his birth certificate with him. Amazingly, Beurling returned to Canada by ship to get the birth certificate, then headed back to Britain once more and applied to the RAF again. Britain was desperately in need of flyers and Beurling did have a pilot's licence, so he was finally accepted. His skills so impressed his instructors that he was recommended for a commission as an officer. However, he turned down the offer, preferring to serve as a sergeant pilot.

In Britain Beurling displayed a knack for two things: shooting down enemy fighters and refusing to follow orders. His "Buzz" nickname came from his habit of flying at top speed over Allied airfields just a few metres off the ground. Anyone in his path had to flatten to avoid being ground into hamburger by his plane's propeller as he "buzzed" them.

In 1942 the British garrison on the Mediterranean island of Malta was under siege by the Italian and German air forces. Beurling requested and was given a transfer to Malta, which was considered by many to be a suicide assignment. He shot down 27 airplanes in 14 days. The press dubbed him "The Falcon of Malta," but his fellow flyers called him "Screwball" because he didn't swear, rarely drank, and refused to socialize with them.

Beurling eventually racked up a total tally of 31 kills and one shared victory. He likely would have scored higher except that when the Battle of Malta was over his reputation for oddness and insubordination caused other squadrons to refuse his requests for transfer. Beurling eventually moved from the RAF to the RCAF and finally accepted a commission as an officer. Gaunt and exhausted, he returned to Canada to participate in a fund-raising drive, but his frank opinions about Allied incompetence and his graphic descriptions of air battles quickly made him a public-relations liability. Beurling returned to Britain but was rarely allowed to fly combat missions again. He was discharged from the RCAF in 1944, a few days before D-Day and at a time when the Allies could have used a pilot with his skills.

After the Second World War, Beurling couldn't settle down to civilian life. With war threatening in the Middle East, he opted to help Israel in its fight for survival against its Arab neighbours in the late 1940s. Beurling died mysteriously in Urbe, Italy, on May 20, 1948, when the Norseman bush plane he was piloting exploded as he attempted to land. Because he was on his way to fly for the fledgling Israeli air force, it is suspected by some people that he was assassinated by the British Secret Service, which supported the Arab nations at the time.

bombers, and escort it to a target over France. Beurling was the lead pilot, and as the new guy, Charley was appropriately Tail-End Charlie. As a sprog embarking on his first combat mission, Charley was determined to show the other pilots he could fly as well as the best of them.

When Beurling signalled the takeoff, all four planes revved their throttles and taxied down the runway together. With all his flying experience Charley had no problem trailing the number three Spitfire tightly, but the pilot in the plane ahead became nervous when he saw Charley tucked so close behind his wing. He was so busy watching Charley that he didn't pay enough attention to the number two plane and almost hit it before they took off. The number three pilot chopped his throttle back, forcing Charley to back off, too. Then the number three revved his throttle to catch up to number two, making Charley do the same thing. Charley was so worried about being left behind on

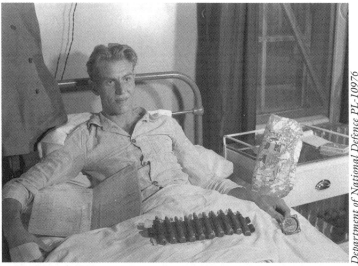

Department of National Defence PL-10976

George "Buzz" Beurling was Canada's top Second World War ace and was Charley Fox's first combat commander. Here he is showing off war trophies while recovering in the hospital after being hurt in a plane crash in Gibraltar.

the runway, the telltale mark of a raw sprog, that he really poured on the gas, causing his Spitfire's tail to rise sharply as the plane's speed picked up.

When Charley heard a brief noise as the Spitfire lifted into the air, he looked out but couldn't see anything wrong. He tested all the controls, and everything felt right at first, but as they crossed the channel he noticed that the beat of the Merlin engine didn't seem quite right.

The American bombers failed to show up at the rendezvous point, so the Spitfires circled, hoping to glimpse a "target of opportunity" — an enemy airplane, or a vehicle on the ground that presented itself by chance for an attack. Unfortunately, no targets of any kind were spotted, so Beurling led the flight back to base. This turn of events was a relief to Charley because his engine was still making strange noises.

FASCINATING FACT
Messerschmitt Bf 109 — Workhorse of the Luftwaffe

The Messerschmitt Bf 109 (also known as the Me 109) had the most prolific production run of any warplane in history. The official records have been lost, but it is believed that between 33,000 to 39,000 109s were manufactured before and during the Second World War. It was also flown by more aces than any other fighter aircraft and was still being piloted as a combat aircraft well into the 1960s, long after its many rivals had been sent to the scrap heap. The Bf 109 was designed by Willy Messerschmitt, a former glider engineer who became friends with high-ranking Nazi Party officials during the early 1930s. After the war, Messerschmitt spent two years in prison for using concentration-camp inmates in his factories as slave labour.

The Bf 109 first flew in combat in 1936 when test aircraft were sent to Spain as part of the Kondor Legion to support the rebel Fascist forces of Generalissimo Francisco Franco. The 109's superior performance against the obsolete biplanes of the Spanish government's Republican military convinced German leaders they had a winning design. The Luftwaffe placed an open order for 109s that eventually ballooned into the tens of thousands.

Fast and nimble, the Messerschmitt also had a reputation as a tricky plane that could easily kill an inexperienced pilot. The aircraft's major weak spot is its tall and narrow landing gear, which makes the plane prone to toppling during takeoff and landing. Some critics claim that more Bf 109 pilots were lost due to crash landings and takeoffs than were killed in combat. In speed and turning radius it is slightly inferior to the Spitfire, but in the Second World War it had a definite advantage over the more numerous Hawker Hurricanes. A series of modifications upgraded the 109 throughout the war and ensured that the plane was never quite obsolete. Even when faster and more modern aircraft were available, many top German aces refused to give up their beloved 109s. These included the world's three top-scoring fighter pilots, all of whom flew 109s: Erich Hartmann (352 victories), Gerhard Barkhorn (301), and Günther Rall (275).

Messerschmitt originally intended his plane to be armed with just three 7.92 calibre machine guns mounted on the fuselage, but when he heard reports that the British were building a fighter with eight .303 machine guns, he fitted his aircraft with a 20 mm automatic cannon that fired through the centre of the propeller. Later versions of the Bf 109 saw two more cannons added to the wings, which gave the aircraft a devastating punch. Some models were even armed with two 210 mm Nebelwerfer rockets to attack Allied bomber formations.

Compared to the Spitfire and most other Second World War fighters, the Bf 109 was cheap to build and easy to maintain. That was why the Germans stuck with the 109 right to the end. After the war, surplus 109s were sold overseas where they became the backbone of many fledgling air forces in the Middle East. Czech-produced 109s, known as Avias, were even used by the Israeli air force in the 1948 War of Independence where they fought against Spitfires piloted by Egyptians. Ironically, as late as 1965, Bf 109s were still part of Spain's air force and were flying the same skies the plane first saw action in back in 1936.

As they landed at Biggin Hill, Charley taxied to the U-shaped earthwork abutment where he parked his Spitfire to protect it from enemy attack. Spinning the plane around, he shut off the engine, climbed out of the cockpit, and noticed something as the propeller came to a slow halt. On RAF airplanes the outside 22 centimetres or so of all propellers were normally painted bright yellow to help ground crew see them when they started to spin. Now, as the propeller blades stopped rotating, Charley saw no yellow tips. Every blade had been sheared off as neatly as if someone had come by with a buzz saw and given them a perfect trim.

The funny noise Charley had heard when he was taking off was the sound of his own propeller blades hitting the runway as his Spitfire's tail rose too fast. He was lucky the wooden blades hadn't shattered as they touched the ground or hadn't dug in and flipped his aircraft, which almost certainly would have been fatal in a fighter plane loaded with fuel and ammunition. Had the flight seen combat against German fighters, Charley

The Messerschmitt Bf 109 was the backbone of the German Luftwaffe. Slightly superior to the Hurricane and slightly inferior to the Spitfire, the 109 was the weapon of choice for many of Germany's top aces, including Erich Hartmann.

would have been easy prey once he attempted to throttle up to full speed. As it was, he was a very lucky sprog who had survived his first combat mission.

Later that evening Charley was surprised when Buzz Beurling asked him to play pool in the recreation hall. When they discovered that the poolroom was empty, Beurling came straight to the point. He told Charley that the wing commander who owned the plane Charley had borrowed was annoyed that the rookie hadn't turned back as soon as a mechanical problem had become a possibility. That was standard procedure.

Charley explained to Beurling that he had thought his reputation would have been forever ruined if he had turned back on his first combat mission because he believed he had a mechanical problem. Beurling listened and nodded. "I'm supposed to give you a reprimand," the ace said as air raid sirens went off and the ominous drone of approaching German bombers

WORDPLAY

Squadron Codes and Aircraft Letters

One Spitfire tends to look pretty much like another. To identify squadrons and even individual aircraft, each plane was assigned letters. A two-letter code was painted in front of the roundel to indicate what squadron it belonged to and one letter was painted after to designate individual aircraft. Charley Fox's fighter squadron, 412, was given the letters *VZ*. A squadron was divided into two or more flights. If a squadron only had two flights, the first was called A Flight, and all the aircraft in that flight received letters from *A* to *M*, while B Flight was given letters *N* to *Z*. Of course, with airplanes being constantly destroyed, repaired, and replaced, individual letters quickly became irrelevant as pilots from different flights had to share Spitfires. So the first flight could take off with letters anywhere from *A* to *Z*.

was heard. Charley and Beurling dived under the pool table. Over the noise of the throbbing bomber engines and the bombs going off all around them, Beurling leaned over and shouted in Charley's ear, "Consider yourself reprimanded!"

Fortunately, Charley's subsequent combat operations occurred without incident. With Beurling leading the way, Charley made many successful runs over the English Channel all the way to France and back. The pilots of 412 Squadron had no way of knowing, but they were helping pave the way for Operation Overlord, the planned invasion of Normandy by the Allies in June 1944. Their operations were designed in part on lessons learned from an earlier landing that had ended in disaster.

In 1942 the Allies had attempted a large-scale raid on the town of Dieppe on the northern coast of France. It was a frontal assault on a prepared enemy position, one of the most difficult types of attack. Canadian troops made up the vast majority of the casualties of the Canadian/British/American strike force. Of the nearly 5,000 Canadian troops who landed at Dieppe, 907 were killed, 2,460 were wounded, and 1,946 were taken prisoner in just nine hours. The RAF and RCAF also suffered defeat above Dieppe as they attempted to protect the Allied troops on the beach below. Between them the RCAF and RAF lost 119 aircraft against German losses of only 46. In this battle Allied pilots encountered a new German fighter — the Focke-Wulf Fw 190.

The main reason for this double defeat was that the raid was so small that the Germans were able to bring in reinforcements quickly from surrounding areas and concentrate their combined power on the Allies to overwhelm them in a matter of hours. Operation Overlord was also going to be a frontal assault on a prepared enemy position just like Dieppe, but the chief difference was that the Allied attack force would be a great deal larger. Also, before the invasion, every effort would be made to prevent the Germans from massing their power against the Allied soldiers as they landed on the beaches.

The first task, though, was to win complete air superiority over the coast of France. Every day squadrons of Allied fighters were sent across the channel to find German airplanes and destroy them. If the Germans were in the air, they were shot down. If they were on the ground, they were destroyed where they sat and the air bases were bombed out of existence. This relentless campaign forced the Germans to pull their airfields farther and farther back from the front lines so that they were harder for the Allies to reach. As it turned out, this action made it equally difficult for the Germans to respond when the Allies unleashed Operation Overlord.

FASCINATING FACT
Focke-Wulf Fw 190 — Butcher Bird

The Fw 190 was a nasty surprise for Allied pilots when it first appeared in the sky in 1941. Powered by a BMW radial engine, the Fw was capable of 610 kilometres per hour in its first model. Unlike the Bf 109, the Fw 190 made takeoff and landing easy for pilots because its wheels weren't as close together. The Fw packed a deadly punch because it was typically armed with two 20 mm cannons and two 13 mm machine guns. Some versions carried four cannons.

The first major combat debut of the Fw 190 was in August 1942 during the infamous Operation Jubilee in which nearly 5,000 Canadian soldiers attempted to raid the French seacoast town of Dieppe. While the Canadian infantry was severely battered on the ground, the Allies took a similar drubbing in the air as a mixed force of more than 300 Spitfires, Hurricanes, Typhoons, and Mustangs tangled with just over 100 Fw 190s. The Allies lost more than 100 fighters and six bombers, while the Luftwaffe lost only 48 fighters. The Fw 190 clearly outclassed the Hurricanes and Spitfires in this battle and quickly earned its nickname "Butcher Bird." Fortunately, British engineers were able to upgrade the Spitfire, and it was soon a match for the 190. Many top-scoring German aces flew 190s. Between them, Otto Kittel (267 victories) and Walter Nowotny (255) downed more than 500 Allied aircraft in Fw 190s, or the equivalent of 26 enemy squadrons.

The Fw 190 was successfully adapted to ground-attack, fight-bomber, and night-fighter roles and was considered one of the best planes of the Second World War. Like the Spitfire and other fighters, it was constantly improved until the final versions were capable of speeds of more than 680 kilometres per hour. More than 20,000 were produced by the end of the war. After the Second World War, the Fw 190 was even employed by Germany's former enemy, France, until the introduction of jet fighters.

The Focke-Wulf Fw 190, one of the best fighter planes of the Second World War, had a devastating effect on the Allies in the air during the ill-fated Dieppe Raid in August 1942. Charley Fox shot a 190 down in December 1944.

German military targets on the ground were also attacked in the same way. Trucks, artillery pieces, tanks, and other vehicles were hammered wherever they were spotted. Once again, to keep from being utterly destroyed, the Germans were forced to move their panzer tank units away from the beach area or disperse them around the countryside in small groups, which made them less effective as fighting units.

Eventually, Charley became an expert at both aerial combat and ground attack. He credits his effective marksmanship to Buzz Beurling. Although Beurling had a reputation as a loner and an oddball, if a new pilot showed a sincere interest in learning how to improve his accuracy, the ace happily spent hours teaching him everything he knew about the advanced technique called deflection shooting.

With his keen eyes and excellent motor skills, Beurling already had a natural talent for gunnery, the military term for hitting a target. But Beurling took it several steps further by mastering deflection shooting, which was aiming not where the target was but where it would be when the bullets were finally in the target's range. Beurling spent hours working out chart after chart of calculations to determine where a pilot should aim depending on his airplane's speed and angle of attack in relation to the enemy's speed and the angle of flight. He even made a little "gizmo" out of rotating pieces of cardboard that a pilot could use with one hand to calculate the proper angle of deflection quickly.

The Spitfire's gunsight at the time consisted of an iron ring with a bead in the middle. To hit a moving target that wasn't flying straight ahead of him, the pilot had to mentally calculate the "angle op," or how many rings (or fractions of a ring) above, below, or left and right he had to lead the target to hit it.

Beurling and Charley spent hours together during which the flight lieutenant called out, "Enemy climbing, left to right, 200 miles per hour. You are closing at 100 miles per hour. What's the angle op?" Charley meanwhile attempted to figure out the right answer and often went to bed with images of Bf 109s and Fw 190s whirling in his head.

The cannons on most Allied fighters were set to fire in a pattern 4.8 metres across, which was like firing a shotgun at an elusive enemy. The pilot fired a big burst and hoped that one of his rounds hit anywhere on the target. Beurling had his ground crew adjust his cannons so that they came together in a spread of less than two metres across. He would never fire his guns until he was sure he was going to make a hit, then would aim at either the wing root (where the wing joins the fuselage) or the cockpit. Charley noticed that Beurling rarely fired more than five or six cannon rounds per burst, but he hit the enemy much more often and always with devastating results.

Although Beurling was the only person who ever mastered his gizmo, Charley learned enough from the flight lieutenant to enable him to usually hit a target when he took aim at it. But with enemy airplanes so scarce at the moment, Charley decided to focus on ground attacks. Again Beurling's lessons paid off. Charley prided himself on his marksmanship and became very skilled at sneaking up on enemy targets and blasting them before they could put up an effective defence. In a matter of a few months he became known as a "train buster" by destroying or damaging more than a dozen enemy locomotives, scores of railway cars, and more than 100 enemy road vehicles ranging from trucks to tanks. Charley became a flight leader (of four Spitfires) that he led across the French countryside on armed reconnaissance search-and-destroy missions.

Attacking Nazi trains wasn't an occupation for pilots with faint hearts or tender nerves, since the Germans mounted lots of automatic anti-aircraft guns on special cars at the front, back, and middle of their trains. The Nazis disguised their anti-aircraft cars to look like normal boxcars, but as soon as an enemy plane was within range, the sides of a "boxcar" dropped

WORDPLAY

Flights, Squadrons, and Wings

When airplanes began flying in formations larger than pairs, new terminology had to be invented to describe them collectively. As usual the Royal Air Force borrowed jargon from the Royal Navy where a small formation of similar-type naval vessels was called a squadron. The basic unit of an air force is a flight or section of three or four (or more) aircraft. Two or more flights form a squadron, which can consist of from 12 to 24 aircraft. Three squadrons (and as many as 10) usually make up a wing. In wartime these numbers always change, since casualties and reinforcements alter a squadron's actual fighting strength almost daily

and the guns began firing. Strafing from any angle often meant that an attacking Spitfire had thousands of cannon shells per minute shot at it. The best train hunting occurred at the break of dawn when hot steam from a fast-moving locomotive left a telltale trail of mist in the cool morning air. These vapour trails could be spotted from kilometres away, giving train busters like Charley a sign to move in for an attack.

If they were lucky, Charley and his flight mates were able to dive on an enemy train, attack, and be long gone before the Germans even knew they were in the area. On most occasions, however, sharp-eyed sentries noticed them before they were within range and then they had to dive through a hail of enemy bullets before they could attack. The Spitfire's 20 mm cannons were dwarfed by the 30 mm and 40 mm guns the German ground gunners used, so Charley and his fellow pilots had to get within a few hundred metres before they could effectively fire their guns.

Charley always led an assault so that he was able to strike the locomotive from the side while the three other Spitfires spread out to the right or left to hit the rest of the train in an extended line. This method prevented German flak gunners from concentrating their fire on any one Spitfire. It also made it difficult to aim their flak guns because they were on a platform moving sideways as they fired. Charley's team strafed the enemy boxcars, trying to detonate ammunition or fuel, while Charley focused on the locomotives, which were expensive and much harder for the Germans to replace than boxcars full of ammunition.

Locomotive boilers were powered by high-pressure steam. One well-placed cannon shell could blow up a boiler, causing a whole train to derail. The German gunners, of course, did their best to make sure Charley never reached their locomotives. Anti-aircraft gunners used special ammunition. One in five bullets was painted with phosphorous, which burns when it comes into contact with oxygen. These flaming bullets, called tracers, were used by both sides to guide automatic anti-aircraft fire toward a target. As Charley rushed in for an attack, it looked as if the Germans were firing red tennis balls at his plane. But he knew that one hit from a "tennis ball" could kill or maim him, or knock his Spitfire out of the air.

The safest ground assault method was for a pilot not to let the enemy know he was going to attack. A favourite technique was to pretend not to see an enemy target and

FASCINATING FACT
Ack-Ack Attack

The Luftwaffe word for ground attack was *Schlacht*, which literally means "slaughter." This concept applied both ways. An airplane diving on an unaware ground target had a great advantage because of the element of surprise. But if the ground target was prepared, the aircraft had the disadvantage

By the Second World War, all armies had developed a branch of the military that specialized in defending ground targets from enemy planes. Anti-aircraft fire was referred to by Allied pilots as ack-ack (from the initials *AA*) or Archie (because soldiers have a way of giving funny names to dangerous things to ease their fear) or flak (from the German word *Flugabwehrkanone*, which means "air defence cannon"). Both the Allied and Axis forces used many types of anti-aircraft guns of different sizes.

In a pinch any standard machine gun works against enemy planes flying at low altitudes. The German MG-42 could throw out a withering 1,200 bullets a minute. For longer ranges the Germans employed 20 mm, 30 mm, 40 mm, and 88 mm cannons. The 30 mm cannon let loose 120 rounds per minute or two per second. That was bad enough, but the Germans built them on special bases that could mount four guns at once. This combination was especially dangerous, since it combined a high rate of fire with a deadly projectile. Some of the trains Charley Fox attacked had as many as eight cannons to protect them. The 40 mm cannon was even more destructive, with double barrels that threw out explosive shells weighing more than four kilograms each. Such cannons had an effective range of 2,200 metres, which meant their rounds could hit enemy planes long before they were in range to do damage to a ground target.

To help with aiming, airplanes and anti-aircraft batteries both used "tracers," special bullets painted with phosphorus that ignited after the rounds were fired. Tracer bullets weren't intended to set enemy targets on fire. Instead they were meant to show gunners where their ammunition was actually going as it flew through the air. Tracers were added to regular rounds usually in a ratio of one in five.

Firing at planes flying at high altitudes required large-calibre guns, since only they had enough power to throw shells straight up thousands of metres. These big AA guns used ammunition that exploded when it reached a certain altitude, sending hundreds of deadly pieces of metal, called shrapnel, in all directions. Fuses were timed so that the projectiles went off after a certain number of seconds, or they were rigged to make sure the shells detonated when they reached an intended altitude. When Allied pilots flew over well-defended German targets, they joked that sometimes the flak was so bad they could step out of their planes and walk home on all the lead being thrown at them.

Department of National Defence

Members of the Royal Canadian Air Force's 412 Squadron take time out from the war to pose on a Spitfire in England in 1944.

then fly away over the horizon, only to return from a different direction a few minutes later, moving low and fast and using trees and hedges as cover. This procedure was called a rhubarb because the pilots flew so low that they felt as if they could reach down and pick rhubarb out of the French farm gardens they hurtled over. A rhubarb attack required exceptional flying skills and pinpoint accuracy. Like Beurling, Charley held his fire until he was sure he could hit the target. The intelligence officers who later reviewed film from Charley's gun camera often remarked that they were amazed at how few cannon shells he used to blow up a target.

At Biggin Hill Charley became friends with Larry Love, a flight sergeant in the 412 with whom Charley shared Spitfire VZ-D. Despite their differences in rank, Charley and Larry became good friends, and on the rare days when they both weren't flying they often borrowed an old British car and went for drives around the English countryside.

Soon, though, such enjoyable jaunts would be a thing of the past. Something big was about to happen, something that would test every soldier, sailor, and pilot to the limit.

7 Invasion

On the morning of June 6, 1944, Charley and his flight mates were roused before dawn and informed that the invasion of France had finally begun. Their mission was to patrol the skies over the landing beaches to prevent enemy fighters or dive bombers from attacking the thousands of Allied troops who would be storming the well-defended beaches below. VZ-D was going to be a very busy aircraft, since both Charley and Larry were scheduled for three flights each that day.

Charley went first. For his initial mission he took off in the dark from southern England. He was flying "spare" — an extra Spitfire that was supposed to turn back if all the planes in the flight checked out to be airworthy once they were in the air. However, Charley knew history was in the making, and he wanted a glimpse of it.

As dawn broke over the English Channel, Charley glanced down and was shocked to see thousands of ships of all shapes and sizes jammed into the channel and sailing south toward France. Looking around, he noticed that the skies were full of Allied aircraft ranging from squadrons of single-engine fighters to full-winged, multi-engine bombers. As his flight reached the French coast, Charley sighted Sword and Juno Beaches where the Canadians and British were about to land. Troop transports and landing craft skittered like water bugs in circles as they waited for orders to go ashore.

Charley's Spitfire rocked from the concussion as the big cruisers and battleships opened fire with their huge guns on the French shoreline, but what really took Charley's breath away were the "rocket ships." They were officially known as LCT(Rs) or landing craft tank (rockets). LCT(Rs) were self-propelled barges originally designed to carry tanks, but hundreds had been converted to lug more than 1,000 12.5-centimetre rockets packed into tubes pointing skyward like rows of organ pipes. Each rocket delivered the explosive power of a single large-calibre artillery shell. When the order was given to fire, the rockets were launched in groups of 20 or more, with the salvos timed fractions of a second apart. With a deafening roar the rockets blasted up off the deck of the barge in a blinding flash of flame and smoke. As they

FASCINATING FACT
D-Day — June 6, 1944

During the dark early hours of June 6, 1944, nearly 7,000 vessels of all types and sizes left their harbours in Britain and stealthily sailed across the English Channel to make a surprise attack on German-occupied France. Code-named Operation Overlord, the D-Day assault was the largest seaborne invasion in history.

The attack was preceded by weeks of heavy bombing and strafing by thousands of Allied planes to disrupt German defences as much as possible. On the night before the amphibious landing thousands of British, Canadian, and American paratroopers were dropped behind German lines to seize strategic points and to disrupt the enemy's communications.

On the first day of the landing nearly 160,000 soldiers from Canadian, British, and American armies stormed more than 80 kilometres of heavily defended beach. The landings were supported by continued bombardment from more than 1,000 naval vessels and around-the-clock bombing and strafing by more than 10,000 Allied airplanes. In addition, 23,400 paratroopers and glider soldiers landed behind enemy lines to seize key bridges and hamper enemy troop movements. By June 19 the Allies had landed more than a half-million soldiers and more than 100,000 vehicles.

The invasion had to be timed just right to take advantage of low tides that would allow the Allied landing craft to avoid beach obstacles and explosive devices that the Germans had placed in the water, expecting the Allies to attack during high tide. The original date for D-Day was June 5, but bad weather forced the Allies to put off the invasion for 24 hours. The forecast for June 6 wasn't much better, so U.S. General Dwight D. Eisenhower, the commander of the invasion, had to make a difficult decision. If he launched the invasion in bad weather, chances were good that it would fail. If he delayed the invasion, it would take several weeks before the tides were favourable again and the element of surprise would be lost. Eisenhower gambled that the weather would clear long enough to make a solid landing, and fortunately for the Allies he was right.

Many people think the term *D-Day* was coined for the June 6, 1944, invasion of France. Actually, it was a standard military term for the designated day a military operation was scheduled to commence and its usage can be traced back to the First World War. However, Operation Overlord's D-Day so caught the world's attention that the term has been associated with the Allied invasion of France ever since.

passed overhead, they sounded like a dozen freight trains. When the rockets struck the shore, they landed the way they were released — close together in clumps that detonated with terrific force.

The rockets were a "surprise" weapon that was so secret that they terrified both the Germans and the Allied soldiers who had never seen anything like them before. A few low-flying Allied planes even collided with the flying bombs and disintegrated. Amazingly, despite the combined bombardment by the air force, navy guns, and rockets, 84 percent of the German artillery and defences remained intact as Allied troops stormed the beaches. Fortunately, because of the lessons learned at Dieppe, the Allied soldiers succeeded in pushing the German defenders off the beach, even though they were launching a similar frontal assault on a well-prepared defensive position. Hundreds of amphibious tanks, close air support, and overwhelming numbers of attacking infantry gave the Allies the momentum they needed to make good their invasion.

Charley had already exceeded his orders by flying across the English Channel, so he reluctantly returned to England to refuel. Larry made his first flight in mid-morning, while Charley took off for his second trip to France in the early afternoon. His flight patrolled the skies over Juno and Sword Beaches, making sure German fighters couldn't attack the British and Canadian soldiers below. Other Spitfires flew close to the ground, acting as spotter aircraft for the naval guns. Even from patrol height, the noise and smoke of battle were clear to Charley and the other pilots. Charley wondered if his brother, Ted, was down there somewhere.

Landing back in England, Charley watched VZ-D take off an hour later with Larry Love at the controls. That was the last he ever saw of Larry or VZ-D. Somewhere over France, Larry became separated from his flight and disappeared. When Larry failed to return, Charley was assigned another Spitfire. It wasn't until 1945 that Charley discovered that Larry had crashed in France and that his body was buried in a small churchyard in Normandy.

Charley flew a third mission in another Spitfire. Just as on his second mission, no German fighters were seen. Allied preparations had worked. The Germans managed to launch fewer than 100 sorties against the entire 80-kilometre front on D-Day. Part of the success was due to deception. Even on D-Day, the Allies sent hundreds of ground-attack aircraft to bomb

WORDPLAY

Aces Have It, or Do They?

Once pilots began shooting down their enemy counterparts in aerial combat, air forces tried to keep accurate records of how many enemy aircraft each pilot destroyed. This policy was partly meant to reward the best and bravest pilots in each squadron and partly to boost public morale at the home front, since the highest-scoring pilots became celebrities the way musicians and film actors are famous today. A pilot who shot down five enemy aircraft was called an ace after the highest value in card games such as poker or blackjack. A particularly notable achievement was to be an "ace in a day," a fighter pilot who shot down five or more planes in one day. Germany's Manfred von Richthofen, "The Red Baron," was one of the first celebrity aces. There is much controversy and dispute over just how many victories many top aces scored in the First and Second World Wars, but Richthofen is generally credited with the most "kills" in the Great War with 80.

There are a number of reasons why it is so difficult to determine exact statistics for aces. Some pilots exaggerated their victories because they wanted the fame and promotions high scores could bring. Others made honest mistakes: an enemy plane diving to escape could look very much like an aircraft that had just been fatally shot up. When hit by enemy bullets, some planes erupted into flames and smoke, but their pilots still managed to nurse them home and land safely. In the First World War both sides required that a pilot actually had to see the enemy plane crash before he was given credit for a kill. In most cases he also had to have another pilot witness the crash to support his claim.

Unfortunately, in the midst of a multi-plane dogfight, it was hard for anyone to keep track of individual aircraft as dozens and sometimes hundreds of opposing planes were diving, climbing, and shooting at one another at hundreds of kilometres per hour. It was also unwise for a pilot to follow his enemy down to the ground just to see a crash. It exposed him both to enemy ground fire and to an attack from enemy aircraft above him. In the heat of battle most pilots had to "shoot and scoot" and hope for the best. If a pilot was witnessed by his comrades shooting up an enemy airplane but no one saw it crash, he was often given credit for a "damaged" enemy. If the enemy plane was trailing smoke and spiralling toward the ground but no one observed it crash, it was credited as a "probable." But a pilot had to have five confirmed "destroyed" to be called an ace.

In the Second World War, accurate reporting improved somewhat when cameras were mounted on the wings or noses of fighter planes to take pictures every time the guns were fired. Many pilots were able to prove their claims after their planes' film was developed and clearly showed enemy aircraft exploding or flying apart, leaving no doubt what had happened.

If a pilot destroyed an enemy aircraft sitting on an airfield, he was given the exact same credit as if he had shot it in air combat because airfields were almost always guarded by anti-aircraft guns. The same victory credit was also given to a pilot if he shot down an unarmed enemy transport or a reconnaissance plane, because these targets were relatively rare and the occasional easy kill made up for all the hard battles pilots experienced for the rest of their scores.

the coastal defences at Pas-de-Calais, the area where Hitler was convinced the Allies would attack. Hundreds of German fighters and dive bombers were ordered to ignore the Normandy landings and stay ready for the "real" attack that never came. The rest of the credit goes to the daring attacks Charley and other Allied pilots had made in the months previous to D-Day. The Luftwaffe had been bled dry of planes and pilots. Its airfields were far inland and its pilots were few. Another lesson from Dieppe had been learned — for a seaborne invasion to succeed, mastery of the air was essential.

After his third patrol in 12 hours, Charley landed the same way he took off — in the dark. He wrote in his logbook: "A long, long day."

Three days after D-Day, Hitler was finally convinced that the Normandy invasion was the real thing and began to order Luftwaffe attacks. Charley's wing spotted eight Junkers Ju 88 bombers attempting to attack Canadian soldiers on Juno Beach and shot down six of them. Charley got in a few rounds, but he didn't do any damage that he could see. The two surviving bombers fled to German-held territory without dropping a single bomb.

On June 18, only 12 days after D-Day, 412 Squadron moved to France. A temporary airstrip had been laid down at Bény-sur-Mer, a few kilometres inland. The horrific fury of the battle was still plainly visible to the pilots as they passed over Juno Beach. Below them, everywhere, were shattered buildings and bomb craters. Burnt-out tanks and landing craft still bobbed in the water. As the engines of the pilots' Spitfires stopped, the thunder of cannons and the crackle of gunfire made it all too clear that the front line was only scant kilometres away.

Because of its central position in the Canadian part of the battlefield, Bény-sur-Mer became the site of a temporary graveyard for Canadian servicemen. As the graves grew from dozens to hundreds, the RCAF pilots received a constant reminder of how much sacrifice was required of their fellow countrymen.

Living conditions in France for 412 Squadron were primitive. Charley and his mates lived, ate, and slept in small tents. Each man had to dig a slit trench just outside because German artillery shells landed daily in the camp and the Luftwaffe tried bombing Bény-sur-Mer whenever it could. With all the heavy equipment moving about, a few rainy days turned

FASCINATING FACT
Top First World War Aces

The records of many First World War fighter aces are much disputed and quite controversial. What follows is a list of the generally accepted victories or "kills" of the top aces for the major combatants in the Great War.

- Manfred von Richthofen (Germany): 80
- René Fonck (France, top Allied ace): 75
- Edward "Mick" Mannock (Britain): 73
- Billy Bishop (Canada): 72
- Godwin Brumowski (Austro-Hungarian Empire): 35
- Francesco Baracca (Italy): 34
- Eddie Rickenbacker (United States): 26

Library and Archives Canada PA-116491

A flight of four Spitfires from the Royal Canadian Air Force's 412 Squadron prepares to take off in formation.

the camp into a mud puddle and a heat wave transformed it into a dust bowl. The Canadians and British were fighting hard to take the French city of Caen a few kilometres away. The Germans were making a stubborn defence at Caen directed by Field Marshal Erwin Rommel, the Desert Fox. Charley's brother, Ted, was part of the battle as his battery of 25-pounder heavy cannons pummelled the deeply entrenched Germans. A good night's sleep was hard to get with the constant thunder of battle in the background, which was often drowned out by the ear-splitting roar of Spitfires taking off and landing.

It was an unpleasant place to be, yet two members of 412 Squadron were voluntarily there when they could have been comfortably back in Canada. Charley finally had his own Spitfire, VZ-F. It came with two ground crewmen — Bill "Danny" Daniels and Murray "Monty" Montgomery. Daniels was in charge of VZ-F's engine, and Monty took care of the plane's airframe. Their duties were to fine-tune the Spitfire's 12-cylinder engine, refuel its gas tanks, reload its weapons, and make sure the plane was in perfect condition every time Charley took off for combat. Because Montgomery and Daniels had been working on Spitfires for nearly three years before they were assigned to Charley's plane, he had great confidence in their skills.

Most of the time the relationship between flyers and their ground crewmen was formal because most pilots were officers and most ground crew members were enlisted men. Charley and his ground crewmen were the opposite. From the day they first met they worked like a team of equals who jointly owned the Spitfire. Monty and Danny fixed the plane, while Charley just happened to be the guy who flew it. But Charley heard that Danny and Monty were due to be repatriated to Canada because RCAF airmen were entitled to go home once they had served three years overseas. Monty and Danny hadn't said anything to Charley, so he thought he would surprise them with a going-away gift. He wrote to his wife back in Canada and asked her to send him two hard-to-find cigarette lighters and have the names of his ground crewmen inscribed on them.

When Monty's and Danny's last day arrived, Charley shook their hands, thanked them for taking such good care of the Spitfire and him, and then gave them the lighters. Charley said that as long as they had been his crew, whenever he climbed into the cockpit, he knew he had no worries. He said he was going to miss them, but that they had done their duty. Almost in unison Danny and Monty said, "Charley Fox, when you finish your tour, then we'll go home."

FASCINATING FACT
Top Second World War Aces

As with First World War fighter pilot victories, the totals for Second World War aces aren't always cut and dried and controversy continues today concerning actual numbers. What follows is a list of the generally accepted victories or "kills" of the top aces for the major combatants in the Second World War.

- Erich Hartmann (Germany): 352
- Ilmari Juutilainen (Finland, top non-German ace): 94
- Hiroyoshi Nishizawa (Japan): 87
- Ivan Kozhedub (Soviet Union): 62
- Marmaduke St. John "Pat" Pattle (South Africa, top Royal Air Force ace): 51
- Richard Bong (United States): 40
- James "Johnnie" Johnson (Britain): 38
- Pierre Clostermann (France, with the Royal Air Force): 33
- George "Buzz" Beurling (Canada): 31 and one shared kill

FASCINATING FACT
Canadian War Cemeteries

So many Canadians were buried at Bény-sur-Mer, France, at the end of the Second World War that it was made a permanent cemetery for Allied servicemen. The vast majority of the 2,049 graves belong to Canadians, with just four British and one French resistance fighter as exceptions. Eighteen of the graves belong to soldiers from the North Nova Scotia Highlanders and the 27th Canadian Armoured Regiment who were taken prisoner by the Hitler Youth 12th SS Panzer Division on June 7, 1944, and executed in violation of the Geneva Conventions. In both world wars Canada didn't bring home its war dead. To save money and preserve morale on the home front, the country buried its fallen soldiers where they died. Hundreds of cemeteries across Europe, Asia, and Africa contain Canada's war dead, which number more than 100,000. In France, Canadian graveyards such as Bény-sur-Mer are meticulously maintained by the French government as a token of gratitude for the tens of thousands of Canadians who died fighting to liberate the country from the Germans. New graves are added nearly every year as more remains of Canadian servicemen are discovered buried in farm fields and construction sites.

Charley didn't know what to say. He had barely started his combat career, which meant Monty and Danny were prepared to spend a much longer time away from their families than they had to. Charley never forgot the sacrifice Monty and Danny made for him, and he credits their expertise, dedication, and hard work as more reasons why he survived the Second World War.

Late in the afternoon of July 17, 1944, 412 Squadron took off from Bény-sur-Mer and flew to Caen. From there the squadron split into three sections of four planes each, with Charley leading his section to patrol the skies over La Roche-Guyon, a village just beyond Caen. They were on an "armed reconnaissance" mission, searching for targets of opportunity to attack and destroy. Far below, something moving fast along a tree-lined country road caught Charley's eye. It was a large, shiny black car, the type often used by high-ranking German officers as their personal transportation.

The car was approaching Charley's squadron at eleven o'clock. Charley didn't want to spook the driver into finding cover, so he radioed his section to keep flying straight as if they hadn't noticed anything. The car continued to race down the road. As soon as the vehicle was out of sight, Charley signalled to his wingman, Lieutenant Steve Randall, that they were descending for a closer look. The two planes made a wide circle and swooped down. Travelling at more than 500 kilometres per hour, they caught up with the vehicle in a matter of seconds, and Charley saw that it was indeed German. With the convertible top down and the rushing wind in their ears, the occupants of the car likely didn't hear the diving planes closing in behind them until it was too late.

With Randall watching his back, Charley concentrated on reducing the distance to his target and waited until he was within 300 metres before he took careful aim through the Spitfire's gunsight and squeezed the trigger on his joystick. VZ-F shuddered as its machine guns and 20 mm cannons spat flame and smoke at the car below. Charley watched his guns send up geysers of dust to the left and side of the car, causing it to veer off the road and crash into a ditch. When it was clear that Charley's attack was successful, Randall and Charley quickly climbed to avoid any hidden anti-aircraft batteries or surprise attack from enemy planes.

Department of National Defence

Members of the Queen's Own Rifles of Canada pay tribute to their fallen comrades at Bény-sur-Mer in Normandy. So many Canadian soldiers were buried here, the landing strip where 412 Squadron was first stationed in France, that the airfield eventually became a permanent Canadian war cemetery.

Compared to the heart-pounding experience of attacking a well-defended army convoy or military train, this "target of opportunity" was easy prey. Charley quickly forgot about the lone car he had left smoking on the ground and resumed his patrol. He claimed another target that day, a mechanical transport vehicle or MTV. When he landed, he recorded in his logbook: "1 staff car damaged." He was unaware that within a few seconds he might have changed the course of the Second World War with just the squeeze of a finger.

A day or two later Allied intelligence reports indicated that Field Marshal Rommel had been seriously wounded by an Allied fighter in a strafing attack. Charley immediately thought of the German staff car he had shot off the road, but he knew the odds of being the pilot

FASCINATING FACT
Erwin Rommel — Desert Fox

Erwin Rommel was one of the most brilliant military leaders on either side during the Second World War. He served with distinction as a German infantry officer in the First World War, and when Germany surrendered to the Allies in 1918, he was one of the few officers kept on in the tiny defence force Germany was allowed to maintain. At the outbreak of the Second World War, even though he had no experience with tanks, Rommel requested permission to lead an armoured division. Because he was a favourite of Hitler and other high-ranking Nazi officials, he was granted command of the 7th Panzer Division and was assigned to take part in the invasion of Belgium and France. Despite his lack of armour training, Rommel led his tanks through a series of dazzling victories against French, British, and Belgian forces until his division was the first to reach the English Channel. His success earned him even more approval from Hitler and made him a military superstar to the German people. At the same time many of his fellow army officers suspected Rommel's victories came more from luck and recklessness than skill in battle.

Rommel proved his detractors wrong in 1941 after he was appointed a division commander of the Afrika Korps, a German expedition sent to Libya to help the Italian army in its losing battle with the British and their Commonwealth allies. The small German division commanded by Rommel independently scored several quick victories that reversed the course of the war in Africa. The British grudgingly dubbed Rommel "The Desert Fox" in respect for his abilities. After the Americans joined the war in December 1941, the Axis armies were eventually pushed out of Africa by superior Allied forces, but Rommel's reputation as a brilliant commander was complete. Returning to Continental Europe in 1943, he was eventually given the important task of supervising the building of coastal defences in northern France against a possible Allied invasion from Britain.

Within a few months of Rommel's arrival in France, the coast of Normandy bristled with millions of mines, kilometres of barbed wire, and thousands of tank traps and concrete bunkers. On June 6, given the poor weather and the fact that it was his wife's birthday, Rommel decided an Allied attack was unlikely and was on leave in Germany. The officers who were left in command were afraid to make decisions, resulting in a fateful paralysis of German ground forces as the Allies landed.

After D-Day, Rommel took command of the Germans defending the French town of Caen. As usual his forces put up a brilliant defence and inflicted many casualties on the Canadian and British armies. But the one thing Rommel couldn't control was the sky. The Germans had lost air superiority over France, and every day hundreds of Allied ground-attack planes patrolled the skies at will, hunting for targets.

On July 17, 1944, Rommel received a fractured skull after his staff car was strafed by a Spitfire and he was thrown against the windshield of his vehicle when it smashed into a ditch. While he was recovering, some German army officers attempted to assassinate Adolf Hitler with a bomb. Although there was no evidence that directly linked Rommel to this plot, he was eventually blamed as one of the ringleaders. Because he was still a hero to the German people, Rommel was forced to commit suicide on October 14, 1944, to preserve his good name and keep his family safe from the wrath of the Gestapo, the German secret police. Rommel's death was blamed on the injuries he suffered from a Spitfire's guns, and he was given a state funeral with Hitler himself participating in the service.

who had wounded Rommel were low. With so many Allied fighters patrolling the skies over France, many German staff cars were shot up nearly every day.

The Americans reported that one of their P-47s had strafed a German staff car on July 17 and immediately insisted they had taken Rommel out of the war. Two days later the Germans confirmed that Rommel had been badly hurt and that the attacking plane had been a Spitfire. Attention then turned to all the Spitfire pilots who had claimed a German staff car on July 17. Besides Charley, a South African air force pilot named Chris Le Roux had also destroyed a German staff car in the La Roche-Guyon area on the afternoon of July 17. But Le Roux's car was in the same vicinity at just after 5:00 p.m., and Charley had been there just after 6:00 p.m. When the Germans stated that the attack occurred at 5:00 p.m., the credit for putting Rommel out of the war was given to Le Roux. Sadly, Le Roux didn't enjoy his newfound celebrity for long. He was killed in a flying accident on September 18, 1944, almost exactly two months after Rommel was strafed.

Charley didn't really care if it was Rommel he strafed over Normandy. The Battle of Normandy was in full swing, and he had plenty of work to do. On an almost daily basis a German tank, transport, or locomotive fell victim to Charley's guns. Eventually, his skill at attacking trains earned him a Distinguished Flying Cross, a medal given for both bravery and talent. Charley's medal came with the following commendation:

Field Marshal Erwin Rommel (left) confers with his superior, Field Marshal Gerd von Rundstedt, who before D-Day was commander-in-chief of Germany's western military forces.

This officer has displayed exceptional courage and skill in pressing home his attacks against the enemy. These operations have been particularly directed against mechanical transport in the course of four consecutive days. Flight Lieutenant Fox destroyed or damaged at least sixty-four enemy transports and since the invasion of Normandy has destroyed a total of 127 vehicles. Many of these attacks were completed in the face of very intense anti-aircraft fire from enemy positions. This record has been a fine example to his fellow pilots and he has contributed much to the success obtained by his squadron.

By December, German fighters were back and Charley got his first real taste of aerial combat. Unlike the First World War when opposing squadrons often broke up into one-on-one duels, most Second World War air battles were like barroom brawls in which fighters wheeled and turned and took quick shots at an enemy, then peeled off before another enemy could fire at them.

Charley's first aerial victory was a Bf 109, which he shot down on a patrol over France on Christmas Eve 1944. His second victory was a Focke-Wulf Fw 190 on December 27, 1944, which was a far more challenging plane to fight. In this incident the Fw 190 attempted to evade Charley's guns by flipping over and diving, but Charley employed a manoeuvre he had practised a hundred times in a Harvard. He flipped over, too, then followed the Fw 190 and actually shot it down while flying upside down!

Two days later Charley damaged a Junkers Ju 88C (a medium German bomber converted to a night fighter) as it was landing at its airfield. Anti-aircraft fire immediately erupted from every gun on the ground, and Charley made a fast

FASCINATING FACT
Distinguished Flying Cross

In all wars that Canada participated in before the 1990s, Canadian military personnel who distinguished themselves in action against the enemy were honoured under the British system of decorations, which included the Victoria Cross and other medals. The Distinguished Flying Cross (DFC) was created in 1918, shortly after Britain's Royal Air Force came into existence. It was originally "granted only to such Officers and Warrant Officers of Our said Forces as shall be recommended to Us for an act or acts of valour, courage, or devotion to duty performed whilst flying in active operations against the enemy." If a flyer won the distinction twice, a Bar was added to the medal. The equivalent medal for Canada's naval personnel was the Distinguished Service Cross, while for the army it was the Military Cross. In 1993 a separate set of Canadian honours for military valour were created by the Canadian government. These are the Canadian Victoria Cross, the Star of Military Valour, and the Medal of Military Valour.

getaway. He was pretty sure the Nazi bomber had crashed, but since every anti-aircraft gunner on the airfield was hoping to get another shot at him, he knew it wouldn't be wise to go back and take a picture. So Charley was given credit for damaging the bomber.

Charley's hard work at the end of 1944 didn't go unrewarded, though. The Allies expected the Germans to take New Year's Day off, so some pilots were allowed to rest and relax. Charley drew the right long straw in a squadron lottery to see who went to London to celebrate the new year and who stayed in France to do routine patrols. A few lucky 412 pilots and crew, Charley among them, partied in London until the wee hours of the morning. While they were still sleeping soundly during the first hours of 1945, the Luftwaffe launched Operation Bodenplatte (Baseplate), the last big attack on the Western Front by the German air force.

Operation Bodenplatte was an effort to kick-start the stalling German land offensive known as the Battle of the Bulge. Just before Christmas, Hitler had launched a massive armoured attack on the U.S. Army in the Ardennes Forest in an attempt to break through to the English Channel and re-create the 1940 success of the Battle of France. When the German ground forces ran out of momentum (and gas), Hitler ordered more than 1,000 German airplanes (mostly Bf 109s and Fw 190s and a few Messerschmitt Me 262s) to attack 17 allied air bases in

For his bravery and leadership in combat, Charley Fox was awarded the Distinguished Flying Cross.

FASCINATING FACT
What Really Happened?

In the 1990s, Michel Lavigne, a Quebec historian, sent Charley Fox a copy of a German report on the Junkers Ju 88C bomber that he had attacked in December 1944 and confirmed that the plane indeed was destroyed. Two of the three German crew members were killed, but Charley was relieved to read that one survived, though he was badly wounded. Had this been known during the war, Charley's score of destroyed airplanes would have been five, which would have made him an ace.

France, Holland, and Belgium. Four hundred and sixty-five Allied aircraft were destroyed or damaged on the ground, and hundreds of airmen were killed by German bombs or the Allies' own exploding fuel and ammunition.

However, the victory was short-lived and costly for the Germans. They lost 304 planes, while 238 irreplaceable pilots were killed or captured. Within two weeks all 17 Allied air bases were up and running at full capacity again, while the German war effort was permanently weakened by the lost pilots and airplanes. Of the 304 German aircraft destroyed in Operation Bodenplatte in 1945, only 62 aircraft were lost to Allied fighters. The majority were destroyed by anti-aircraft gunners. As a further insult, 84 of the German aircraft were knocked down by "friendly fire" flak. To preserve the element of surprise, German anti-aircraft crews weren't informed about the raid, so they opened up on their own Luftwaffe comrades both on the way to the Allied airfields and on the way home.

The Luftwaffe pilots were so demoralized by their losses during the raid that several top aces confronted Hermann Göring, leader of the Luftwaffe, and accused him of wasting their lives needlessly. Instead of listening to their complaints, he demoted all of the "mutineers" and sent them back to serve as mere pilots, thereby depriving the Luftwaffe of many of its best squadron commanders when it needed them most.

The Allies had delivered crushing blows to the Germans, but the Nazis weren't kayoed yet. They had a lot more surprises in store for Charley and his compatriots.

8 Buzz Bombs, Bogus Fighters, and Bad Weather

Both the Allied and German air forces were grounded in late December 1944 during the first week of the Battle of the Bulge. When the weather cleared in January, both sides scrambled to get their planes into the air to grab superiority over the battlefield and to assist their respective armies on the ground. The RCAF sent up four squadrons to sweep the sky for German fighters. Charley was leading his flight of four Spitfires on the extreme right when he spotted six aircraft abreast about 1,700 metres below and to the right of his formation. A long, thin cylinder projected under each wing of the unidentified aircraft, convincing Charley that he was looking at a flight of Me 262s, the new German jet fighter that could fly much faster than any plane the Allies had over Continental Europe.

Charley called out to Wing Commander Blair Dalzell Russel, "Six jets, two o'clock below." Russel ordered Charley's flight to "Get into them," so Charley immediately led his pilots in a dive to attack the fighters from behind. The 262s continued in a straight line, which Charley thought was strange, but he wasn't going to take any chances. Once the 262s were aware of the Spitfires on their tails, they could easily accelerate and escape.

With the targets flying so straight and level, Charley struck from 1,000 metres. That was an extreme range, but attacking the enemy planes was like shooting sitting ducks who weren't making any attempt to evade their foes. With the momentum from the 1,700-metre dive

FASCINATING FACT
Me 262 and the Gloster Meteor — Arrival of the Jet Age

The Second World War saw the introduction of jet fighter planes on both sides of the conflict. Sir Frank Whittle of Britain and Dr. Hans von Ohain of Germany are acknowledged as having invented nearly identical jet engines in the 1930s. Whittle, however, had great difficulty in convincing the British government to fund his research. He even lost his engine patent because he didn't have enough money to pay the annual £5 renewal fee. By contrast, in Germany, von Ohain was hired by airplane manufacturer Ernst Heinkel, and in August 1939 the Heinkel He 178 became the first operating jet plane in history. Although this jet reached a top speed of more than 650 kilometres per hour, military experts remained skeptical, especially after the aircraft nearly crashed on its second flight when a bird was sucked into the plane's engine.

After the outbreak of the Second World War, both Germany and Britain poured money into jet development. The first combat jet in history to go into action was the British Gloster Meteor, which flew its initial military operation on July 27, 1944. The Messerschmitt Me 262, the Germans' first operational jet fighter, appeared in the skies shortly after the Meteor in August 1944. The Nazis claimed that 19 Allied planes were destroyed by their experimental jets in that first month, though this assertion has never been completely verified.

The rival jets resembled each other in many ways in their first versions. Both were single-seat, twin-engine fighters armed with four cannons in the nose. The Me 262 had a range of about 1,000 kilometres and a service ceiling of 11,500 metres, while the Meteor's range was around 1,600 kilometres and its service ceiling was 12,190 metres. However, the Me 262 had a significant advantage in speed and climb rate over the Meteor. The German jet was capable of 870 kilometres per hour and could climb at 20 metres per second, while the Meteor could only achieve 660 kilometres per hour and had a climb rate of 11 metres per second.

The two aircraft were fated never to meet in combat due to the vastly different roles assigned to each plane. With their superior speed Meteors were detailed to protect Britain from V-1 flying bombs. The British also wanted to keep their precious jets away from the front line in case one fell into the hands of the Germans.

Adolf Hitler had personally hindered Willy Messerschmitt's development of the Me 262 by insisting on a high-speed bomber, not a fighter. Messerschmitt humoured the Führer by producing a bomber variant while concentrating on the fighter version dubbed the "Swallow," named after a very fast and agile bird.

The Germans eventually produced more than 1,400 Me 262s, but only a fraction could take to the air at once due to fuel and parts shortages and constant airfield attacks by Allied fighters. The British did eventually move a few Meteor squadrons to the front lines, but the war ended before they could make a difference in the outcome. Improved versions of the Meteor served with the Royal Australian Air Force in the Korean War. Nearly 4,000 were eventually produced.

assisting it, Charley's pilots closed in quickly on the 262s and opened fire. Charley saw his bullets strike his target on the right wing. Bits of metal flying off told him he was hitting his target. Then a big section of the wing sheared off, and the enemy plane immediately tilted over and went into a steep dive toward the ground. Charley thought it was odd that the German pilot didn't try to bail out.

As soon as the first plane was hit, Charley expected the whole German flight to break off and accelerate. Curiously, though, the 262s continued in a straight line as if nothing had happened. When Charley lined up his sights on the next plane, he spotted a big scoop as part of the fuselage of the enemy aircraft. To his horror, he realized he hadn't just shot down a German Me 262 but an American-built P-51 Mustang fighter. What he had believed was the aircraft's jet engines were, in fact, long-range gas tanks that P-51s carried so they could fly escort with bomber flights for the full distance from Britain to Germany and back.

The Messerschmitt Me 262, the aircraft of the future, soars through the air. Fortunately for the Allies, the Germans got this jet into combat too late in the Second World War for it to make a significant impact.

Charley shouted, "Don't fire! Don't fire!" and ordered his flight to break off its attack immediately. As they climbed to rejoin their wing, they watched the Mustangs carry on, oblivious to the fact that one of their planes was now missing. Wing Commander Russel later agreed with Charley that from above the P-51s had looked exactly like Me 262s. Both of them were puzzled by the behaviour of the Mustang pilots. Sometime afterward, Charley heard that the Germans were experimenting with remote-radio-controlled planes. To prevent losing their own fighter planes in crashes or from being shot down, the Germans used captured Allied aircraft to test their new gadgets. Charley still hopes that this was the case with his mysterious P-51 encounter.

Earlier in the war Charley had a near-fatal meeting with another baffling airplane. In mid-September 1944 he was flying alone over Holland. Far below, Operation Market Garden was underway. The Luftwaffe was sending out wave after wave of fighters and bombers with orders to destroy a series of bridges held by Allied paratroopers behind German lines.

FASCINATING FACT
Operation Market Garden

Operation Market Garden, unleashed in September 1944, was an ambitious plan devised by British Field Marshal Bernard Montgomery to burst through the German defensive line in Holland by concentrating armour and infantry in one powerful spearhead that would stab through with an unstoppable force. The Germans had a natural advantage: eight rivers blocked the Allied line of advance and each one was a barrier to the attacking forces. There were lots of bridges over each river, which the Germans were still using for their defence needs. However, the Allies knew if they approached the bridges the Germans would immediately blow them up and use the rivers as natural moats. Montgomery's scheme was to land thousands of airborne soldiers by parachutes and gliders along a highway that led into Holland. The airborne soldiers would seize the bridges from the Germans before they could destroy them and then hold them until the main body of Allied troops arrived. Unfortunately, Montgomery's strategy proved to be too complicated and was dogged by bad luck. Most of the bridges were successfully seized by the Allies, and some units held them for as long as nine days, but the main Allied force couldn't break through and drive far enough to link up with the paratroopers. Of the roughly 10,000 Allied paratroopers who participated in Market Garden, more than two-thirds became casualties, more than 2,000 were killed, and 6,000 were taken prisoner. *A Bridge Too Far* (1974), the non-fiction book by Cornelius Ryan, documents Operation Market Garden in all its harrowing detail. In 1977 the book was turned into a movie of the same title directed by Richard Attenborough and starring Robert Redford, Anthony Hopkins, Michael Caine, Dirk Bogarde, and James Caan.

It had been a busy four days for 412 Squadron, which had 31 destroyed enemy fighters and seven probables to its credit. Charley had become separated from his wingman during an encounter with a flight of Bf 109s and Fw 190s. Low on fuel and ammunition, he was heading back to Bény-sur-Mer when he noticed another lone Spitfire approaching. Charley wiggled his wings, convinced that it was his missing wingman. The Spitfire closed rapidly as Charley leisurely zigzagged in case any hidden AA guns were trying to draw a bead on him. Fortunately, he glanced back to see where his wingman was. The man was supposed to be beside him. Instead the Spitfire was behind him. Then, just as Charley looked back, his "wingman" opened fire on him!

Immediately, Charley pulled back on his joystick to dodge the spray of bullets and to show the other pilot the unmistakable elliptical wing of his Spitfire with its red-and-blue RAF roundels. Charley did a complete roll, straightened out, and resumed flying toward Normandy. He glanced back and saw that the other Spitfire had circled to come in from behind again. Charley threw his joystick over to the left and began a series of aerobatic manoeuvres as the other Spitfire's guns burped cannon shells at him. Now Charley could see that the attacking plane was indeed a Spitfire, but it had no markings, just a coat of camouflage paint. The aircraft was obviously a captured Spitfire being flown by a German pilot. The duelling planes were perfectly matched, and so were the pilots. The German and Charley went around and around, each trying to gain an advantage on the other.

Charley had one major disadvantage: he was already low on fuel and ammunition when he was ambushed by the phony friend. He managed to manoeuvre the other pilot into a head-on attack, which meant that the planes were hurtling toward each other at more than 500 kilometres per hour. When the other Spitfire was within gun range, Charley let loose the last of his ammunition, then ducked under his opponent at the final second. He had no idea if he had hit the other Spitfire, but he kept going so that by the time the enemy Spitfire turned around, Charley was already kilometres away. Running on fumes from his gas tank, he safely returned to Normandy.

Later in the war Charley learned that Sandy Borlan, a fellow RCAF Spitfire pilot from Guelph, was shot down by an unmarked Republic P-47 Thunderbolt in similar circumstances. The P-47 was the largest fighter airplane of the Second World War and was hard to mistake for anything other than what it was. Borlan recognized the aircraft as an American-made fighter and allowed it to approach unchallenged. Without warning the P-47 opened fire on Borlan and he was killed.

Shortly after D-Day, the Allies were surprised by a strange flying bomb that "buzzed" when it flew. It was called the V-1, and as long as people could hear it buzz, they were safe, since that meant the bomb was still flying. When the engine stopped, people learned to duck and hold their breath, knowing that the bomb had run out of fuel and was now falling toward the ground. The bombs carried enough explosives to destroy several large buildings at once and leave enormous craters. The windows on buildings a half-kilometre away would crack from the detonations.

The Allies responded by setting up a multi-layered defence of fighters, anti-aircraft batteries, and balloons. Squadrons of Typhoon, Hurricane, Spitfire, and Mustang fighters were deployed to intercept the V-1s, also known as buzz bombs or doodlebugs, and shoot them down before they reached Britain. But that was extremely hard to do. The flying bombs cruised at more than 600 kilometres per hour, close to the top speed of most Allied fighters

FASCINATING FACT
The Doodlebug — Hitler's Vengeance

After the Germans lost air superiority to the Allies, they became more desperate and inventive in finding ways to attack their enemies. Adolf Hitler ordered his scientists to produce *Vergeltungswaffen* (vengeance weapons) to wreak terrible vengeance on the Allies. The first to see service was a flying bomb called the Vergeltungswaffe 1 (Vengeance 1), also known as the Loon by the Germans. The V-1 could fly at 640 kilometres per hour and fall to earth at nearly 800 kilometres per hour. The flying bomb carried 850 kilograms of high explosive to a maximum range of just over 320 kilometres. Its "pulse-jet" engine made an unfamiliar buzz that caused the Allies to nickname the weapon the buzz bomb, the farting fury, or the doodlebug (Australian slang for the antlion, an insect that makes a buzzing noise with its wings; in its larval stage it "doodles" in the sand as it builds its nest).

The V-1 was a simple but effective weapon. With only a rudimentary guidance system the Germans couldn't aim the rocket bomb very accurately. They could only launch it in the general direction of the enemy and try to time it so that the fuel ran out when it was over the target. Then it would fall to earth and explode. The point of the V-1 was not to bomb military targets with precision but to terrorize British civilians as payback for the horrors Germany's civilians experienced from day and night Allied bombing. The first V-1 was launched against Britain on June 13, 1944, just a week after D-Day. Another 10,000 doodlebugs followed, but thanks to Allied air defence, bad weather, and mechanical failures of the bombs, only one-quarter of the V-1s launched made it to England. However, the ones that did hit London destroyed almost as much property as all the German bombs during the Blitz. They also killed more than 6,000 people and injured almost another 18,000.

Several of the best German test pilots were killed trying to land piloted versions of buzz bombs after testing their flying characteristics. Hanna Reitsch, Germany's only female test pilot, successfully landed the buzz bomb because she already had experience in the Messerschmitt Me 163 Komet rocket fighter. The Germans sent a V-1 engine to Japan, which the Japanese adapted to power a flying bomb piloted by a suicide bomber. The Japanese called the flying bombs "cherry blossoms" to reflect the samurai spirit, but the Americans dubbed them baka bombs, *baka* being Japanese for "moron."

After the Second World War, France, the United States, and the Soviet Union developed their own versions of the V-1. The buzz bomb is considered to be the ancestor of the modern cruise missile, developed and still used by the United States.

Other *Vergeltungswaffen* projects of the Germans included:

- V-2, a ballistic rocket that was impossible to shoot down with airplanes or anti-aircraft guns because it fell noiselessly from the stratosphere.
- Messerschmitt Me 262 jet fighter.
- Messerschmitt Me 163 Komet, a rocket-powered fighter plane. It flew at nearly 960 kilometres per hour, but unfortunately ran out of fuel in eight minutes, then the pilot had to glide down for an unpowered landing.
- V-3 Super Cannon, a huge smooth-bore gun designed to lob 600 tonnes of high-explosive shells at London daily.
- Panzerkampfwagen VIII Maus, a barn-sized super tank with the cute Nazi nickname "The Mouse."

The V-2, Me 262, and Me 163 were produced successfully, but fortunately for the Allies they were introduced into service too late to affect the outcome of the war.

of the time. V-1 attack fighters were specially modified for maximum speed by removing their armour plating and anything else that slowed them down. Then the fighters had to be already in the air and close to the flight path of the bomb, since there was no time to chase it over a long distance. Because the buzz bombs tended to cruise at altitudes of 600 to 900 metres, Allied pilots patrolled several thousand metres higher so that they had a better vantage point to spot incoming bombs. Also, at that height, when they dived, the fighters had the benefit of the additional speed provided by the force of gravity.

The next challenge was to knock the buzz bombs out of the sky. V-1 fuselages were made of steel, which deflected bullets at long and medium range. Fighters had to get within a few hundred metres to hit the bombs hard enough to detonate them with bullets. However, if the fighters successfully pierced the V-1s, the resulting massive explosion could easily destroy them, too. It took a lot of courage and composure for a pilot to chase and shoot at an object he knew might blow up in his face and possibly kill him. Several Allied pilots died this way, including Free French ace Jean-Marie Maridor.

If a V-1 was over the English Channel or British countryside where it could do little damage if it crashed, some pilots "tipped" the bomb instead of shooting at it. Bomb tipping involved carefully flying up beside the doodlebug until the plane's wing tip slid under the V-1's wing. Then the pilot tipped the bomb's wing upward. When the V-1 was tipped, its delicate balancing mechanism failed and the bomb spun earthward. This method, too, had its perils. The steel buzz bomb was heavy and had plenty of inertia in flight, while Allied fighters were made of lightweight aluminium, wood, and canvas. It was easy to bend or even break off a plane wing trying to tip a doodlebug.

Despite the dangers of bringing buzz bombs down, some pilots became quite skilled at it. The most famous V-1 ace was Flight Lieutenant Joseph Berry who, while flying a Hawker Tempest, destroyed 61½ doodlebugs, including seven that he dispatched in a single night. Berry later died after being shot down by a German sentry during a ground attack on a radar station over Holland. He was 24.

The next line of defence against buzz bombs was anti-aircraft guns. The Germans had chosen the V-1's low cruising height because they knew anti-aircraft gunners would find the bombs difficult to hit. The range was too low for large AA cannons and too high for small AA machine guns such as quad-fifties (four .50 calibre machine guns). V-1s were also hard to track as they streaked overhead.

Fortunately, Allied anti-aircraft defence had come a long way since the Battle of Britain in 1940. The Allies now coupled advanced radar tracking with their AA guns so that they could spot and aim at incoming V-1s before the bombs even appeared on the horizon. Special fast-moving gun mounts built by the Allies enabled AA gunners to move their barrels quickly to keep targets in sight as they flew by. Finally, the Allies had a secret weapon of their own — anti-aircraft shells with proximity fuses. With proximity fuses, artillery shells didn't have to strike targets. They just had to get close and then they would detonate. These improvements enabled the Allies to destroy as much as 80 percent of incoming V-1s by late 1944.

The final line of defence was balloons. More than 2,000 huge balloons were deployed like a flying hedge between London and the V-1 launching sites. Long, heavy wires were suspended from each balloon to cut the wings of buzz bombs passing underneath. The Germans countered by installing wire cutters on the leading edges of the V-1's wings, but more than 300 doodlebugs were brought down by the balloons.

Of course, the best way to defeat buzz bombs was to prevent them from being launched. Fortunately, V-1s were fired from large ski-jump-style ramps easily visible from the air. The Nazis built more than 100 sites along the coasts of France and Holland with the intention of launching 1,000 V-1s a day. Although the Germans tried to camouflage their launch pads, photos from Allied reconnaissance planes and information from spies working for the French and Dutch Resistance identified most of the V-1 sites almost as soon as they became operational.

One day Charley Fox was ordered to lead a flight of Spitfires on a dive-bombing run against a V-1 base in Holland. The launchers were typically located in a grove of trees, but the telltale clues were a long concrete slab with railway tracks leading up to the 50-metre-long ramp. Another clue was the ring of 40 mm AA positions around a supposedly pastoral scene. Even if pilots couldn't see the ramp, the hail of red tracers erupting out of the trees announced there was a target worth attacking.

Spitfires weren't designed to be dive bombers. Dive bombers were slow, but they had heavy reinforced fuselages capable of withstanding tremendous G-forces as the planes dived straight down, released their bombs, then pulled up to avoid colliding with the ground. The more delicate Spitfires had to "dive" from a gentler angle or else their airframes could break from the G-forces and crash.

Charley led his flight in for the attack in a typical Spitfire "loop" assault, diving from a high altitude and releasing the bombs so that they were lobbed horizontally at the target. The Spitfires then veered away, making sure they were well out of range before their bombs detonated. Charley and his mates had the element of surprise and were able to complete their bombing run and duck over the horizon before the defenders had a chance to zero in on them.

Unfortunately, Charley's 227-kilogram bomb had failed to release. The German gunners were now on full alert. Every instinct told him he should fly away, try to shake the bomb loose over the English Channel, and go home. For all he knew the bomb might not release on the second run. If he attacked again and were hit, he would be too low to bail out and would crash into the ground with an armed bomb strapped to his plane. But then Charley thought about what his father would do in the same situation and knew William Fox would finish the mission even if it cost him his life. Charley radioed to his section to stay out of ack-ack range while he went in to drop his bomb.

On most other missions Charley didn't think about the danger until after he landed and had time to ponder what he had experienced. This occasion was one of the few times he felt his feet shake on the rudder pedals as he spun his Spitfire around and returned to the target

Department of National Defence PL-42109

Flight Lieutenant Charley Fox (left) relaxes with his wing and squadron commanders in Holland in 1945.

where the gunners were alert and waiting for him. The red tracers began arcing skyward as he pushed his joystick forward for the attack. The German gunners were likely expecting a typical loop run, so Charley made an unusual spiral dive toward the V-1 ramp. At the last second he pressed the release lever, and thankfully this time the bomb dropped. A loud explosion momentarily drowned out the pounding bark of the AA guns as Charley opened his throttle to full power and zigzagged away, tracers still chasing him. Somehow he escaped unscathed, but he hoped he would never have to taste fear as deep as that again.

Despite the constant menace of anti-aircraft fire, Charley's closest call happened because of a bit of bad timing during a train assault. He was leading a section of Spitfires searching for targets over Germany. When a long train chugging through the countryside was spotted, Charley signalled his mates that they were going to attack. He and his wingman dropped to the deck and hedgehopped toward the target. The Germans spotted them and were waiting with their guns locked and loaded. Charley dodged the ack-ack and fired a concentrated burst into the locomotive, but nothing happened. Now intent on escape, he flew low right over the locomotive to make himself a hard target for the German gunners. Just as the tail of his Spitfire passed over the locomotive, the boiler exploded in a massive blast. Charley felt his plane shudder as if its tail had been hit from below by a huge hammer. German tracers were flying all around, so he tried to bank and dodge, but suddenly his tail controls were gone. His elevators felt sloppy, and he had no rudder command at all!

With tracers still flashing past his aircraft, Charley struggled to prevent the stricken plane from smashing into the farmland below. He slid back the canopy to bail out, then realized he was too close to the ground for his parachute to open. If he leaped out now, it would be like jumping out of a car travelling at 400 kilometres per hour. Carefully, he pulled back on the joystick and was relieved to discover the Spitfire responding sluggishly. At least now he had some control — the ailerons on his wings could make the airplane climb and turn in a limited manner.

But without elevators and a rudder he was unable to zigzag, which made him an easy target for ack-ack. Charley felt as if every long-range 88 mm gun in Europe was pointing at him as he coaxed his stricken Spitfire to climb slowly so he could bail out. He had to be careful not to stall the aircraft by climbing too quickly. If he stalled without working elevators, he would never regain control of his plane as it went into a spin. If he went into a spin, it would be almost impossible to parachute because the corkscrew motion of the airplane would pin him against his seat with multiple G-forces. As black puffs of smoke exploded around him, Charley at least knew he was safe from enemy fighter attack, since his section was flying protective zigzags above him.

The flak decreased as Charley climbed, and he reconsidered bailing out over enemy territory. He had no desire to spend the rest of the war in a German prisoner of war camp. Slowly, he adjusted the joystick so that the plane's nose pointed toward his home base in Holland, hoping he could reach Allied lines before he had to jump.

The memory of the injuries he had suffered from his first parachute jump returned as he crossed into Holland. He recalled the forest rushing up at him and the jarring impact when he crashed into the trees. Now he glanced down and saw lots of trees and buildings to hit. He also spied big ponds and rivers where a flyer could drown if he got tangled up in his parachute lines in the water.

When Charley glimpsed the runway of his airfield, he wondered if he could make a safe landing with only his ailerons for control. He followed another Spitfire in a long, slow circle to line up with the runway. Both planes backed off on the throttle and decreased altitude. Charley felt like a waiter balancing a huge tray of easy-to-tip glasses as he tilted the aileron controls so that they turned the Spitfire in a protracted circle. As his Spitfire entered the other plane's slipstream, it rocked and tipped.

By radio, Charley told the pilot in the other Spitfire to land and then get out of the way because he was coming in with a crippled aircraft. A sudden crosswind made Charley's touchdown even more challenging. He corrected his direction by using the wheel brakes and came to a halt at the very end of the runway in a tight semicircle.

After he climbed out of the Spitfire, Charley and his squadron mates checked out the tail of his plane and discovered that the exploding locomotive boiler had completely severed the wires connecting his rudder to the cockpit and that his elevator control was hanging by its pulley.

A high-ranking RAF officer, Group Captain Gordon McGregor, had also witnessed the landing. He asked for Charley's logbook and wrote in a "green endorsement," a rare RAF award that noted the date, time, and number of the aircraft and then briefly described what the pilot did and under what circumstances. This was an RAF tradition, not an RCAF one, so Charley was one of few RCAF pilots to win this commendation.

Around the same time Charley also received a Bar to his Distinguished Flying Cross. A Bar meant that you had been awarded the medal twice. Charley's rising scores were listed in the Bar commendation:

> Since August 1944, this officer has led his section against a variety of targets often in the face of intense anti-aircraft fire. He has personally destroyed twenty-two locomotives and thirty-four enemy vehicles, bringing this total to 153 vehicles destroyed or damaged. In addition, he has destroyed at least a further three enemy aircraft and damaged two others. In December 1944, Flight Lieutenant Fox led his squadron on an attack against enemy airfields in the Munster area and personally destroyed another hostile aircraft, bringing his total to four. Through his quick and accurate reporting a further four aircraft were destroyed. Since the award of the Distinguished Flying Cross, this officer has continued to display outstanding skill, coolness and determination.

The Germans were in retreat everywhere, but the closer they got to their homeland the more determined and dangerous they became. In late January 1945, 412 Squadron was moved to Nistelrode, a Dutch town near the German border. With flights going out almost every day, Charley had already racked up nearly enough missions to become eligible for his ticket home.

Often the most hazardous but often unmentioned important air missions in the Second World War were weather checks. Allied commanders needed accurate information about weather conditions before they sent planes in to attack the enemy. Weather checks frequently meant taking off, flying, and landing in poor weather, ranging from fog and low ceilings to rain and snow. With all his instructors' weather flying experience, Charley was one of the best bad-weather pilots in the wing. So when the High Command asked 412 Squadron to send out someone to do a weather check on a terrible day, Charley was usually given the mission.

On January 18 low clouds cancelled the regular missions at Charley's airfield in Nistelrode, but the order came in for

FASCINATING FACT
Seeing Red

The Royal Air Force had a term it called a Red Endorsement. If a pilot was careless and damaged his aircraft without a good reason, a senior officer wrote a negatively worded note in the pilot's log in red ink. If the incident was very bad, the officer sent the offending pilot to a six-week-long "Bad Boys" course to improve his flying skills. More than one Red Endorsement could get a pilot grounded for the rest of his career.

someone to fly to the front lines along the Rhine River to see what the weather was like there. Charley took off but climbed to just over sixty metres because that was where visibility ended. If he went any higher, he might get lost or even crash into a hill or a tall building. From Nistelrode he followed the highway south to Nijmegen, an ancient city close to the German border. One of the main branches of the Rhine flows from Germany into the Netherlands through Nijmegen, so when Charley spotted the river he knew he had to stay west of it to avoid going over the lines and straying into German airspace where hundreds of AA guns likely waited for him. He flew south toward Cologne where the Allied armies were pushing back the Germans.

After Charley made all his weather notes and decided it was time to return to base, he trailed the highway north from Cologne to Eindhoven. When he reached Eindhoven, the weather was still clear enough to continue flying at treetop level, so he remained below the cloud ceiling and proceeded to 's-Hertogenbosch where he knew he could follow the local roads back to Nistelrode.

Charley's Spitfire was so low that he found himself flying between high-rise buildings in 's-Hertogenbosch. When he spied railway tracks, he knew that the eastbound line would take him straight back to his airfield. His guide points would be two tall factory smokestacks that would tell him he was nearly home. But there were two sets of train tracks heading east. Charley followed both of them until he came to a fork and had to choose which one to continue along. He picked the track that seemed to go in an eastbound direction to Nistelrode. As far as he could tell, the other one veered southeast toward Germany.

The countryside below was blanketed in snow from a recent storm, and many rivers were covered in ice. After about 20 minutes, Charley saw the two smokestacks. He made a 180-degree turn around the stacks, knowing that would bring him into perfect alignment with the end of the runway. Flying straight and slowly descending, he was relieved to be home and was looking forward to a hot cup of coffee when an anti-aircraft artillery shell suddenly exploded below his wing in a big black puff of smoke. Shrapnel tore holes in the Spitfire's

WORDPLAY

Variable Pitch Propeller

One of the biggest improvements in aircraft design during the Second World War was the variable pitch propeller (VPP), a Canadian invention created by Wallace Rupert Turnbull (1870–1954). Turnbull was born in New Brunswick and worked with other great inventors, including Thomas Edison and Alexander Graham Bell. In 1922 Turnbull patented a propeller design that allowed a pilot to adjust the pitch of the plane's propeller for maximum efficiency. The invention was successfully tested in 1927. Each blade on a propeller is like a little airplane wing, and its efficiency at pushing air backward to give the aircraft thrust depends on the angle (or pitch) at which the blade is set. But, like the gears on a bicycle, the efficiency of the pitch is also affected by the speed the plane is travelling. When starting off, the pitch is set at a shallow level similar to the lowest gear on a bike to get the vehicle moving. As the plane picks up speed, the pitch is increased so that more air is forced through without overworking the engine or stalling the aircraft. At the beginning of the Second World War aircraft had propellers set at fixed pitches that provided good, if not great, thrust at all speeds. But planes fitted with variable pitch propellers soon appeared, and these aircraft could go faster, higher, and even farther than their opponents because the pilots could adjust the pitch of their propellers to get maximum efficiency. Another advantage of VPP was that if one engine went out on a multi-engine aircraft the propeller on that engine could be "feathered," which meant that the blades were set to cause minimum drag. This ability made flying a disabled plane much easier. Nowadays propellers are so advanced that the pitch can actually be tuned to provide reverse thrust when an airplane lands, something that is especially useful for short-takeoff-and-landing aircraft since it allows them to stop quickly and safely on a very short runway.

wings, another piece knocked out a chunk of the plane's propeller base, and hydraulic fluid that controlled the pitch of the propeller sprayed back over the windscreen.

Charley pulled up into the clouds briefly to throw the flak gunners off, then slowly descended again before he got lost. His windscreen was coated with a film of thick, greasy black oil that was almost impossible to see through. The Spitfire was still flying, but its 12-cylinder engine now made high-pitched screams because the propeller blades had locked into "full fine pitch," forcing the engine to race flat out. Charley knew his plane wouldn't last long taking that kind of punishment.

Instead of cursing German flak gunners, Charley started cussing the Canadian Army. He was sure the shell that had hit him had been armed with a proximity fuse. Only Allied gunners had those, so he suspected he had been nailed by a shell fired by a trigger-happy gunner from his own side. It would be a pretty lame way to end the war to be shot down by fellow Canadians. Once again he thought about his brother, Ted, who was in the Canadian artillery. Perhaps it was his brother's unit that had attacked him. Even the skies of Europe weren't big enough for two Fox brothers!

But if that was Canadian artillery that had clobbered him, Charley realized he now had to fly south to find his airfield. He checked his compass and turned in that direction. In a matter of minutes he crossed a wide river that he recognized as the Rhine. Now he was really confused. Slowly, it dawned on him that the twin smokestacks he had seen must have belonged to a *German* town. That meant he had accidentally crossed the Rhine and that the anti-aircraft shell had come from a German 88, not a Canadian AA gun. But that also meant he was now hurtling over German territory in a badly damaged Spitfire. He veered north again, crossed the Rhine, and kept going until he was reasonably certain he was over Holland.

The weather was deteriorating now, so Charley had to fly even lower while trying to see through the oily windshield. His engine was overheating, and he had only about 20 litres of fuel left. Down below was mostly farmland, so he selected a field with a farmhouse at the end and made a belly landing with his wheels up. As soon as the Spitfire touched down, the propeller blades bent, the engine stopped, and Charley glided through the snow on an aircraft toboggan. He prayed hard that the Spitfire wouldn't dig in and flip. If that

A Spitfire from Charley Fox's squadron finds itself in a Dutch farm field in 1944 after an emergency belly landing. Charley's last combat flight ended with a landing like this.

happened, he might get trapped beneath the aircraft, which would be real bad if the plane caught fire. Fortunately, the Spitfire merely slid to a halt, and Charley was able to climb out unhurt.

It took more than eight hours to hitchhike back to his base. As soon as he walked in, the group captain said, "Charley Fox, that's your last combat mission."

Before Charley could say anything, the wing commander at the next desk said, "Aye. Absolutely."

Just like that Charley was no longer a combat pilot. He wrote in his logbook: "Crash landed. Hit by Flak. And How!"

As soon as Charley was taken out of combat, his world became a little smaller when his ground crew friends, Danny Daniels and Monty Montgomery, applied for and were granted permission to return to Canada. Charley keenly missed them, but they had stayed away from their families seven months longer than they had to just for him, and he knew he owed his life to their skills and dedication.

Relieved from combat, Charley was posted to other duties. He was sent to Heesch, Holland, where he served as a test pilot for 410 Repair and Salvage Unit. His job was to fly Allied aircraft that had been repaired after they were badly damaged in accidents or battle. Charley missed his friends in 412 Squadron, so he applied to be sent back to do whatever the unit could find for him. An opening came up for an operations officer with 126 Wing, and Charley gladly returned to his former unit.

In May 1945, 412 Squadron moved to Wunstorf, a German town in Lower Saxony. On the night of May 4, 1945, Wing Commander Geoffrey Northcott walked into the officers' mess

FASCINATING FACT
Liberation of Holland: A Very Canadian Victory

The Netherlands, or Holland, was invaded by Nazi Germany on May 10, 1940. The tiny Dutch army, armed with outdated weapons, put up a brave resistance, but was ruthlessly crushed by the massive German blitzkrieg. After the bombing of Rotterdam by the Germans, Holland surrendered rather than see the Nazis completely destroy its cities and towns as they threatened to do. What followed was five long years of brutal Nazi occupation. Three-quarters of the 140,000 Jews who lived in Holland were killed in concentration camps (among them Anne Frank). All Dutch males between the ages of 18 and 45 were forced to work as slaves in German factories turning out war *matériel* for the Nazis. Millions of tonnes of food and other goods were stolen by the Nazis and shipped to Germany, resulting in thousands of Dutch civilians starving or freezing to death for lack of food and fuel.

When the Allies began forcing the Germans to retreat after D-Day, by chance it was the Canadian Second Division that was given the task of wresting the Netherlands from German control. The Nazis had fortified their defences in Holland, and Adolf Hitler had ordered his army to hold "Fortress Holland" at all costs. During the bitter struggle, the Germans deliberately opened dikes and allowed thousands of hectares of Dutch farmland to flood in order to prevent the Canadians from advancing easily over the open fields. Eventually, the Canadians prevailed, and the last of the German-held parts of Holland were liberated on May 5, 1945, when the Germans were ordered to lay down their arms.

Of all the Western European nations that endured Nazi occupation, Holland suffered the worst by far, with the highest per capita death rate and destruction of property by war or flooding. Canada's sacrifice for the Netherlands has never been forgotten by the Dutch. Canadian flags are waved by Dutch children every May 5 Liberation Day, and visiting Canadian veterans and their families are given a hero's welcome. In 1945 Holland also sent Canada 100,000 of its finest tulip bulbs, one of the country's national symbols, in gratitude for Canada's sheltering of Dutch Princess (later Queen) Juliana and her children after the Netherlands fell to the Nazis. Since then, every spring, Ottawa holds the world's largest tulip festival as a tribute to an international friendship that was forged in war and that continues to be celebrated with flowers.

of 412 Squadron, stood on a chair, and called for silence. When he had the room's full attention, he read out a message that had come in from 83 Group Headquarters to all units of the RCAF: "All hostilities on the second front will cease at 0800 hours tomorrow, May 5, 1945." The pilots cheered and shook one another's hand. They had survived the European war!

As a fitting close to the war, Wing Commander Geoffrey Northcott decided there should be one last combat mission by 126 Wing on May 5, 1945. At 6:30 in the morning four pilots climbed into their Spitfires for the final combat flight of the war. It was a very senior section. Leading it was Northcott, followed by Squadron Leader Bill Klersy of 401 Squadron and Squadron Leader Don "Chunky" Gordon of 402 Squadron. Tail-End Charlie was scheduled to be Captain Dave Boyd, the commanding officer of 412 Squadron, but Boyd

Thousands of unidentified allied aircrew perished during the war. Here, just days after the Dutch city of Eindhoven was liberated from the Nazis in September 1944, two Canadian airmen place flowers on the grave of a fallen comrade. The grave is marked Unbekannt, *Dutch for "Unknown."*

FASCINATING FACT
Tragedy of War Goes Beyond Surrender

Although they survived the war in Europe, two of the four members of Charley Fox's Last Patrol died from war-related causes soon after VE Day. Squadron Leader Bill Klersy was killed on May 22, 1945, during a patrol when the Spitfire he was flying near Wessel, Germany, hit a hill hidden by a cloud during bad weather. Squadron Leader Donald "Chunky" Gordon died in 1948 from complications due to flak wounds he suffered while shooting down two enemy fighters during Operation Bodenplatte, the 1945 New Year's Day German offensive.

had celebrated a little too hard the night before and didn't feel rested enough to pilot a Spitfire safely. Even though Charley wasn't supposed to fly any more combat missions, he was asked to fill in for Boyd. Charley climbed into Spitfire VZ-F and took his place on the runway.

At 6:15 a.m. the four Spitfires roared down the runway in echelon right formation and rose together into the morning sky. They climbed to patrol height and began a sweep over the German countryside, "looking for the elusive Hun," as Northcott joked. Technically, Germany was still at war with the Russians, so there actually was a small chance they could encounter an enemy fighter formation, but fortunately no German aircraft took up the challenge. The four veteran flyers enjoyed a leisurely flight, then landed at Wunstorf without incident just after 8:00 a.m. They had taken off in war and landed in peace. The last Allied aerial combat patrol on the Western Front was over. Charley Fox finished the Second World War where he had started — as Tail-End Charlie in a section of four Spitfires.

9 Surviving Peace

One morning, a few days after the official end to the war in Europe, Charley was finishing a night shift as operations officer when he heard an unfamiliar engine approach the air base at Wunstorf. He went outside and saw an unmarked "short-nosed" Fw 190 land on the runway. The Fw 190 taxied to a halt, and a German sergeant pilot climbed out. As the senior officer on duty, it was Charley's job to take him prisoner. With the war now over it was more of a ceremony than an arrest, and the German prisoner seemed perfectly comfortable enjoying a cigarette provided by his former enemies.

With the Focke-Wulf sitting on the runway, Charley suddenly got the urge to fly the German fighter plane. The 412's officer of maintenance was from Kitchener, Ontario, a city where a large population of German Canadians lived, so he was able to speak fluent German. The German pilot gave Charley a verbal checkout on the 190 by speaking through the interpreter, but either by accident or design he neglected to mention that the Focke-Wulf's undercarriage could only be retracted by pressing two separate controls. Charley took off, but he couldn't retract the wheels and undercarriage, which made the 190 hard to fly at slow speeds.

As he was coming back in to land, he discovered that the Focke-Wulf also didn't handle well in a crosswind. The German plane had a large tail but a relatively small rudder, which meant that when the crosswind pushed the tail to the side it was hard to compensate by turning the rudder. Charley later discovered that German Fw 190 squadrons tended to use grass fields for runways so they could take off and land into the wind, but Allied pilots didn't know this until after the war. When he landed with a bounce, Charley attempted a correction with the brakes, but they locked up and he almost performed a "ground loop," a sarcastic term used to describe a sprog losing control of his plane and spinning out of control. Never in all his Dunnville days had Charley ever come close to executing a ground loop, but now as a senior officer he nearly did one with half his squadron and a former enemy watching. He wrote in his logbook: "Fw 190. Loud Motor. Lousy Landing."

Charley shrugged off his embarrassment and later flew the Focke-Wulf a half-dozen times more. It became *his* 190 until he was ordered to go home. As a fighting machine, the "Butcher Bird" impressed Charley. It was fast and manoeuvrable, but what really set it apart from other aircraft was the fact that its cockpit was so close to the nose that he found he could fly lower than in any other plane he had flown. "It would make a good lawnmower," he joked to his squadron mates.

Italy and Germany had surrendered, but Japan still stood defiantly at war alone in the Pacific Ocean. The Allies had pushed the Japanese back, but as with the Germans, the closer the Allies got to the homeland the more determined the enemy became. In June 1945 the Americans seized Okinawa from the Japanese, but it cost them more than 50,000 casualties. The toll on the Japanese was 66,000 dead and more than 100,000 civilian casualties. The Allied military experts estimated that, based on Okinawa, it would cost as many as a million Allied casualties to take the Japanese mainland.

Charley had been eligible to go home since January 1945 after completing 100 combat missions, but he had stayed in Germany because he had felt a sense of duty to see the war through with all his friends. In July officers from all three squadrons of 126 Wing went to their group captain, Gordon McGregor, and volunteered to fight in the Pacific theatre if he would serve as their leader.

"Sorry, boys," McGregor replied. "We're slated for occupation."

That meant that instead of fighting against the Japanese, 126 Wing had been ordered to stay in Germany and maintain the peace until stable civilian rule returned to the devastated country.

Later that same day Charley met with McGregor again to make sure the occupation posting was final. McGregor said it was. Charley remembered that he had a wife at home whom he hadn't seen in 19 months and a son he had never seen at all. "I've been pretty lucky," Charley said. "I guess I'd better head home."

McGregor nodded. "Yes, you'd better start signing out."

Charley spent the next day filling out paperwork and collecting the signatures he needed to be sent home. On the morning of July 25 he empted the cannon shells out of the ammunition magazines in his Spitfire's wings and replaced them with his clothes and gear. Then, climbing into the plane, he waved one last time to his friends and took off for England. At Bognor Regis Station on the south coast of England, Charley turned in his Spitfire.

Department of National Defence PL-33171

The Germans also suffered extensive casualties during the Normandy invasion. These are just a few of the 77,866 German graves in France and Holland.

After a night's sleep, he caught a train west to Bournemouth where he boarded the SS *Louis Pasteur* on July 26. The news of the day was that three world leaders, Winston Churchill of Great Britain, Harry Truman of the United States, and Chiang Kai-shek of China had announced that unless Japan, the last remaining Axis enemy, proclaimed unconditional surrender, it would face "prompt and utter destruction" from the Allies. Japan was clearly losing the war, but it was putting up such a dogged resistance that many returning soldiers

FASCINATING FACT
Louis Pasteur Captured in Canada!

The SS (Steam Ship) *Louis Pasteur* was a French ocean liner designed to rival the *Queen Mary* and *Queen Elizabeth* in the luxury tourist trade of the 1930s. It had the misfortune of being launched in the spring of 1940 just as the Germans were closing in on Paris with their panzers. Because of its high speed, the *Louis Pasteur* was loaded with 213 tonnes of gold bullion from the French gold reserves, which it rushed to safety in Canada. By the time the *Louis Pasteur* landed, it was technically an enemy ship because it now belonged to the Vichy French, who were allies of the Germans. As the liner docked in Halifax, a small party of Canadian sailors and officials "captured" it. The gold was off-loaded, and the *Louis Pasteur* was immediately drafted into service as a troop ship. The *Louis Pasteur* transported tens of thousands of soldiers across the Atlantic Ocean — Canadian and American service people east on their way to Europe, and thousands of Italian and German prisoners west to be settled in prisoner of war camps such as the one Charley Fox and his friends buzzed near Dunnville, Ontario. After the war, the *Louis Pasteur* was returned to France where it received that country's Croix de Guerre for its services. The *Louis Pasteur* continued to be a troop carrier into the mid-1950s as France attempted to maintain its hold on its colony in Indochina by shipping thousands of French soldiers there to fight the Vietminh. After France was ousted from Vietnam, the military no longer needed a long-distance troop transport, so the *Louis Pasteur* was sold to Germany where it was finally refitted to be the luxury liner it was meant to be. It served the transatlantic route until the decline of steamship travel and was reduced to being a lowly floating barracks for migrant workers in Saudi Arabia. The *Louis Pasteur* escaped the final indignity of being broken up for scrap when it snapped its tow lines and sank in the Indian Ocean while being hauled to the breaking yards in Taiwan.

wondered if they would be called back to serve in the east, as well. While Charley was crossing the Atlantic Ocean and thinking of home, half a world away a new weapon, the atomic bomb, was being dropped on the Japanese cities of Hiroshima and Nagasaki with devastating results. The "prompt and utter destruction" of Japan had begun.

Charley landed in Halifax and travelled by train to Toronto where he was met by his wife and his son, Jimmy, on August 13, 1945. Their concern about Charley having to someday serve in the Pacific theatre ended the very next morning when they heard on the radio that Japan had accepted the Allied terms of unconditional surrender. Charley returned with Helen and Jimmy to Guelph where both their families lived. The Fox clan was doubly blessed when Ted Fox came home safe, as well.

Although Canada had escaped the devastation that had wracked Europe and many other parts of the world, Charley could still see signs of the war that had happened so far away and yet had affected Canada profoundly. Some were silly things, like the fact that automobiles looked old because the manufacturers had switched to turning out tanks and trucks for the past four years. Women wore homemade dresses and painted their legs with brown dye because stockings were no longer available in the stores since all the nylon was being used to make parachutes and other military gear.

It was still hard to get butter, sugar, and gasoline because rationing was still in effect. People had to present government coupons when they wanted to buy coffee, tea, and meat. But these were minor inconveniences compared to the human toll the war had taken on Canada. Every family in the country had been touched by the Second World War in some fashion. Out of just over a million people who had enlisted to serve for Canada, 46,777 were killed in action or later died of their wounds. Another 53,145 were wounded,

FASCINATING FACT
Rationing Is Good for What Ails You

During the Second World War, though Canada produced a lot more food than it could consume, rationing was introduced because millions of tonnes of commodities were exported to feed Canadian service people overseas plus the civilian populations of Britain, the Soviet Union, and many European countries as they were liberated from the Nazis. Sugar was the first staple to be rationed in Canada in August 1942 and the last one to stop being rationed in November 1947. Other items rationed included butter, gasoline, meat, tea, coffee, chocolate, molasses, cigarettes, and alcoholic beverages. Civilians were issued ration books with coupons that limited how much each person was allowed each month. Although Canadians disliked having limits set on their consumption, government studies found that the general health of Canadians actually improved during rationing, since they were forced to limit their intake of high-calorie foods, to cut down on unhealthy habits like drinking alcohol and smoking cigarettes, and to walk or to ride a bike instead of driving a car for short trips.

some so badly they were doomed to spend the rest of their lives as patients in veterans' hospitals. Others spent years learning to cope with missing limbs or having their faces rebuilt with plastic surgery after being horribly disfigured by burns. Another 8,271 were taken prisoner and many had endured inhuman conditions at the hands of the Japanese and Germans.

At first jobs were scarce because the thousands of businesses that had been turning out *matériel* for the war suddenly had to shut down and retool for the civilian market. When men signed up to serve in the war, they were guaranteed that their jobs would be given back to them when they returned. Often those jobs were gone by the time they got back because the factories had moved. In other cases the people who were doing those jobs during the war (many of them women) were now out of work.

Charley, like most returning servicemen, found it difficult to talk about the war to anyone who hadn't been there, too. Civilians just didn't understand. The government, to keep up the morale of Canadian civilians, had often portrayed the war in a positive light. According to the newsreels that played in the theatres every week, war was an adventure and the Canadian men and women who were serving overseas were having a good time. When a solider died or was wounded, it was for a "glorious" cause. While Charley and the other veterans agreed that defeating the Nazis and Japanese had been a necessary evil, they knew from experience that there was nothing glorious about watching a good friend or a relative die a horrible death.

The Canadian military was shrinking to its old, much smaller pre-war size. The government was closing down scores of Second World War airstrips, and the training aircraft, some brand-new, were being sold for scrap or left to rot in vacant fields. Because of his years of experience as an instructor, Charley was asked if he wanted to continue serving in the RCAF. He wished to keep on flying, but after being away from home so long, he was sure that Helen wanted him to leave the RCAF so they could live the normal routine of a typical Canadian family.

Charley declined the offer, resigned from the air force, and began looking for a job in retailing, which was what he had done before the war. He returned to Walker Stores, Limited, a department store in Guelph. One day the mother of Andy Howden entered the store. Andy was one of the "Four Guys from Guelph" Charley had had his picture taken with in Bournemouth, England. Unlike Charley, however, Andy hadn't come home. On April 7, 1944, Andy and his navigator had taken off in an RCAF Mosquito fighter bomber for a night flight and had simply disappeared.

As soon as Mrs. Howden saw Charley, she started to cry. She walked up to him and began pounding him on the chest, screaming, "Why my Andy and not you?"

All Charley could say was: "Mrs. Howden, I don't know why not me." To Charley Mrs. Howden's grief was understandable and justified. Secretly, he often felt guilty about surviving the war when so many of his friends had perished.

On another occasion, in 1946, Charley was working in the store when a stranger entered. Charley instantly identified the man as a burn victim, very likely from the war. The stranger's face was badly scarred, but there was something familiar about him immediately. As the man approached, Charley recognized the rolling gait of the Ping-Pong shark he had once shared a bunk bed with in Brandon, Manitoba. "Larry!" Charley cried. "Hello, Fat Stuff!"

Larry Summers held out his hand, and Charley shook it.

Like Wally Floody, Larry had become a Spitfire pilot after he shipped out of Dunnville. He had been shot down over German-occupied France. Larry's Spitfire had caught fire on the way down and his face was badly burned before he could bail out. After recovering in a German Luftwaffe hospital, Larry was transferred

> **FASCINATING FACT**
> **A Star Is Born**
>
> The American name for the T-33 jet trainer was the Shooting Star. Canada changed the name of its version to the Silver Star in honour of the Silver Dart, Canada's first heavier-than-air aircraft, one of whose designers was Alexander Graham Bell. The Silver Dart was piloted by John McCurdy and flew in Baddeck, Nova Scotia, on February 23, 1909, marking the first controlled powered flight in Canada and the British Empire.

to Stalag Luft III where he had rejoined Wally. Returning to Canada, Larry had decided to take advantage of a government program to send veterans to school and had applied to the Ontario Veterinary College in Guelph. Larry had walked into the store not expecting to see Charley but recognized him right away. He was thrilled that Charley had known who he was, too, without being told.

It turned out that Charley's wife wasn't as anti-military as he had thought. When he mentioned that he missed flying, Helen said she had really enjoyed the service part when they were living as newlyweds in Dunnville. When Charley was overseas, she had dreaded the thought that like so many other young brides, one day a telegram would arrive informing her that Charley had been killed, wounded, or captured. Now that he was home she thought that the military life was fine — at least on a part-time basis.

Charley rejoined the RCAF in 1954, became a pilot and flying instructor in 420 Squadron, a reserve unit, and flew everything from Chipmunk trainers and P-51 Mustangs to T-33 Silver Star jet trainers. The air force reserve filled a need in Charley to do something with all the experience and training he had received during the Second World War.

10 Charley Fox Today

For the next few decades Charley divided his time between retail work and flying for the air force reserve. In all those years he rarely talked about his many war experiences to anyone except other veterans. The unpopular Vietnam War in the 1960s and early 1970s created an anti-military attitude in many parts of North America. Soldiers were often portrayed as war lovers in movies and television shows of the era, and many Second World War veterans felt as if they couldn't talk about their experiences without being accused of being a supporter of what was going on in Vietnam.

Charley also became active in restoring Second World War aircraft. In 1985 a group of veterans and history enthusiasts in southwestern Ontario started the Canadian Harvard Aircraft Association (CHAA), a non-profit organization dedicated to saving Second World War RCAF training aircraft. The CHAA spent thousands of hours and many thousands of dollars restoring Harvard, Yale, and Tiger Moth aircraft at its headquarters in Tillsonburg, Ontario. At the CHAA Charley met Robin Barker-James, a local teacher who thought students should do more than just read about history in books.

Barker-James owned a farm near the CHAA airfield where he created a medieval village so that his elementary school students could learn about life in the Middle Ages. He also built a replica of the Canadian trenches in the First World War where up to 200 students at a time could learn what conditions were like for Canadian soldiers by digging new trenches, drilling with wooden rifles, and wearing the helmets and battledress of soldiers of that era. Barker-James even managed to get the CHAA to fly over the fields while the students were studying trench warfare to give them a sense of what being in a battle was like.

In 1995, when Barker-James found out about Charley's Second World War experiences, he asked him to come to his school and speak to his students. Charley agreed, but he wasn't sure what to expect. Would the students be bored? Would they be hostile to an old warrior talking about shooting down airplanes and blowing up trains? To Charley's relief he was not only enthusiastically welcomed by the students but they kept him there an extra hour asking him question after question.

When other teachers in the same school district heard about Charley's presentation, his phone began to ring. He received invitations from Rotary Clubs, local history associations, and air shows across Canada to come and speak.

Charley retired from retail sales in 1990 and, other than D-Day, he has never been busier. Not only does Charley speak about his own war experiences, but he has taken on several other projects that are of personal interest to him.

One is to have Second World War flying instructors recognized as full-fledged veterans. Despite the dangers they faced on a daily basis and also the fact that they had no choice whether they went overseas or stayed behind to instruct, Canadian pilots who didn't serve outside Canada during the Second World War are still treated as "second-class" soldiers by the Canadian government. There were no medals for being flying instructors, and there are fewer government medical benefits available to these brave flyers. Charley wants this situation changed immediately while there are still flying instructors around to receive their just recognition and benefits.

A second project of Charley's is to have all Canadians who served as prisoners of war to be recognized as heroes and receive medals. Much as flying instructors were, Canadian POWs were treated like second-class soldiers when they returned from the Second World War. Several of Charley's best friends were prisoners of war, including Walter Floody, Larry Summers, and Steve Randall, Charley's wingman on the day he shot up the German staff car.

All Canadian POWs endured months and even years of harsh conditions as prisoners. Some, especially those who were captured by the Japanese, were routinely beaten, starved, tortured, and denied medical treatment. Even in the German camps, Canadian prisoners who tried to escape were beaten, tortured, and shot. Some were even sent to concentration camps. Many of these men are now suffering extra medical problems directly related to what they endured as prisoners of war. Charley is working to get the government to recognize the heroism of Canadian POWs from all recent wars. He would like to see extra medical benefits granted to all Canadian military personnel who were prisoners of war and wants such people to be granted a POW medal in recognition of their service.

Charley is also lobbying the Canadian government to commemorate the 50 Allied airmen who were executed on Hitler's personal order after the Great Escape. Six Canadians, including Flight Leader Pat Langford, one of Charley's fellow flying instructors at Dunnville, were among the victims. Charley would like to see a special memorial held on April 29, 2010, which would be the sixty-fifth anniversary of the liberation of the prisoners of Stalag Luft III.

The third major project Charley is working on is to have the Canadian government and its Second World War allies recognize the extraordinary achievements of thousands of Polish servicemen who served in the Royal Air Force and alongside the Canadian Army during the Second World War. The RAF's 303 Polish Squadron scored the highest number of victories during the Battle of Britain. On the ground Polish army units fought side by side with Canadian ones. Polish soldiers helped win the Battle of Monte Cassino in Italy from January to May 1944, and they suffered horrific casualties blocking the German army's retreat through the Falaise Gap.

The motto of 303 Squadron was "For Your Freedom and Ours," and yet at the end of the war the Allies allowed the Soviet Union's leader Joseph Stalin to set up a puppet regime in Poland. Furthermore, Polish veterans were denied pensions or even official recognition that they had fought in the war. Because Canadian and Polish military units served together in many theatres of war, Charley wants the Canadian government to take the lead in having the sacrifices of the Free Polish forces acknowledged.

On April 30, 2004, for Charley's long service on behalf of Canadian veterans, he was made honorary colonel of 412 Squadron, his old unit, which is now based in Ottawa. Also in 2004, the controversy over who shot up Field Marshal Erwin Rommel's staff car resurfaced. Michel Lavigne, a Quebec-based Canadian historian, has written numerous books about the Second World War. As part of his meticulous research, he spends hours studying both German records from the Second World War and the official RCAF files at Library and Archives Canada in Ottawa. After each mission, pilots were required to fill out logbooks, which were carefully copied by air force clerks into the official records. Lavigne noted that the time of Charley's attack on a Nazi

In Ottawa in 2004 Lieutenant-Colonel Charley Fox is named honorary colonel of 412 Squadron, now stationed in Canada's capital.

Department of National Defence

staff car entered in the RCAF files and the times documented by German survivors of the Spitfire attack on Rommel's staff car matched exactly.

Charley's personal memory of the attack mirrors German eyewitness accounts of how the Spitfire attacked after swooping in from a nine o'clock position. Still, Charley wasn't prepared for the notoriety, both positive and negative, that arose from Lavigne's conclusion. Suddenly, there were phone calls from newspapers and radio reporters who wanted to talk to the "pilot named Fox who got the Desert Fox." There were also people who accused Charley of trying to "steal" credit from other pilots who also claimed to be the ones who had knocked Rommel out of the war. The Canadian Forces have accepted Lavigne's conclusions and now credit Charley with the attack on Rommel, but there will likely always be counterclaims by other military scholars.

Letting the historians do the fighting, Charley stays out of the controversy. He knows he destroyed a German staff car on July 17, 1944, in the same area where Rommel was known to have been strafed. The historical records seem to agree that Charley was in the right place at the right time, but even an attack on Rommel was merely one tiny incident in a huge battle.

Mixed feelings about Rommel also trouble Charley from time to time. Allegedly, the Desert Fox was involved in the planning to assassinate Hitler on July 20, 1944. What if Rommel really did have a role in the attempt and he hadn't been badly injured three days earlier? Would the plot to kill Hitler have succeeded?

"There's no use worrying about 'what ifs' in war," Charley says today. "What if, instead of instructor school, I was sent straight overseas like most other pilots? What if I was shot down? What if I had just disappeared over the English Channel? What if I had crashed and burned or was captured? The important thing is not to worry about what might have happened but to concentrate on what really did occur. I hope we never have another war like the Second World War, and one of the best ways to make sure that doesn't take place is to remember what actually did happen to thousands of young Canadians who never returned. They are the true heroes of the war."

Epilogue

Once, in the early 1950s while driving home from work on a cold winter night, Charley was about to crest an icy hill near London, Ontario, when he smelled airplane gasoline, oil, and river water exactly like the time he walked into the funeral director's morgue in Dunnville when he had to identify the bodies of Norman Kirk and Tom MacIntyre. Charley hit the brakes and slowed his car to a crawl. As he crested the hill, he saw that the road was blocked by a truck that had skidded. Had he kept on driving the way he was, Charley would have hit the truck full speed and likely died. Charley isn't a man given to believing in ghosts, but he can't explain how that smell suddenly came to him and saved his life.

In 2005 Charley met Bill "Danny" Daniels for the first time in 60 years in Kelowna, British Columbia. In 2007 Charley helped put engines in six T-33s that had been restored in Ontario and they should be flying in 2008.

Flight Lieutenant Charley Fox's official war record included the destruction

FASCINATING FACT
Charley Fox Graduates High School in 2007!

Although Charley Fox had picked up his two missing high-school credits in 1939, he never got around to graduating officially until Clarke Road Secondary School in London, Ontario, granted him a diploma in recognition of all the visits he had made on behalf of Second World War veterans. Charley received his high-school diploma in 2007, nearly 70 years after he finished school. Now that's focus!

of 22 enemy locomotives, 34 military vehicles, and 97 other vehicles for a grand total of 153 ground targets damaged or destroyed. Charley is also credited with four enemy airplanes destroyed and five damaged, though Michel Lavigne has since found an official German report that states that one of the aircraft Charley "damaged" was also destroyed. Unofficially, Charley is an ace. Among other awards he received the Distinguished Flying Cross and Bar. He continues to be active in school visits, air shows, and speaking on behalf of Canadian service people across Canada.

Selected Reading

Barris, Ted. *Behind the Glory: Canada's Role in the Allied Air War*. Toronto: Thomas Allen, 1992.

Berger, Monty. *Invasions Without Tears: The Story of Canada's Top-Scoring Wing in Europe During the Second World War*. Toronto: Random House Canada, 1994.

Beurling, George, and Leslie Roberts. *Malta Spitfire: The Buzz Beurling Story*. Toronto: Penguin, 2002.

Bishop, Arthur. *The Splendid Hundred: The True Story of Canadians Who Flew in the Greatest Air Battle of World War II*. Toronto: McGraw-Hill Ryerson, 1994.

Bishop, William A. *Winged Warfare*. Toronto: Collins, 1976.

Bowyer, Chaz. *Supermarine Spitfire*. London: Arms and Armour Press, 1980.

Dunmore, Spencer. *Above and Beyond: The Canadians' War in the Air, 1939–45*. Toronto: McClelland & Stewart, 1996.

Glancey, Jonathan. *Spitfire: The Biography*. London: Grove Atlantic, 2007.

Granfield, Linda. *High Flight: A Story of World War II*. Toronto: Tundra, 1999.

Hehner, Barbara. *The Tunnel King: The True Story of Wally Floody and the Great Escape*. Toronto: HarperCollins, 2004.

Johnson, James E. *Wing Leader*. Toronto: Stoddart, 2000.

Lyall, Gavin, ed. *Freedom's Battle, Volume 2: Voices from the War in the Air, 1939–45*. London: Vintage, 2007.

McIntosh, Dave. *High Blue Battle: The War Diary of No. 1 (401) Fighter Squadron, RCAF*. Toronto: Stoddart, 1990.

Miller, Douglas. *You Can't Do Business with Hitler*. New York: Little, Brown, 1941.

Nichol, John, and Tony Rennell. *Tail-End Charlies: The Last Battles of the Bomber War, 1944–45*. London: Penguin, 2005.

Nolan, Brian. *Hero*. Toronto: Lester & Orpen Dennys, 1981.

Pigott, Peter. *On Canadian Wings: A Century of Flight*. Toronto: Dundurn, 2005.

Stacey, C.P. *The Half-Million: The Canadians in Britain, 1939–1946*. Toronto: University of Toronto Press, 1987.

Selected Websites

Aero Space Museum of Calgary: *www.asmac.ab.ca.*

Atlantic Canada Aviation Museum, Halifax: *http://acam.ednet.ns.ca.*

British Columbia Aviation Museum, Sidney, British Columbia: *www.bcam.net.*

Canadian Air Aces and Heroes: *www.constable.ca/openingpage.html.*

Canadian Aviation Historical Society, Toronto: *www.cahs.ca.*

Canadian Aviation Museum, Ottawa: *www.aviation.technomuses.ca.*

Canadian Harvard Aircraft Association, Tillsonburg, Ontario: *www.harvards.com.*

Canadian Museum of Flight, Langley, British Columbia: *www.canadianflight.org.*

Canadian Spitfire Restoration Project, Comox, British Columbia: *www.y2kspitfire.com/index.html.*

Canadian War Museum, Ottawa: *www.civilization.ca/visit/cwmvisite.aspx.*

Canadian Warplane Heritage Museum, Mount Hope, Ontario: *www.warplane.com.*

Commonwealth Air Training Plan Museum, Brandon, Manitoba: *www.airmuseum.ca/homebase.html.*

Comox Air Force Museum, Comox, British Columbia: *www.comoxairforcemuseum.ca.*

Dunnville Airport Museum, Dunnville, Ontario: *www.dunnvilleairport.com/museum.php.*

Eshott Airfield, Northumberland, England: *www.eshottairfield.co.uk/?page_id=3.*

Nanton Lancaster Society Air Museum, Nanton, Alberta: *www.lancastermuseum.ca*.

National Air Force Museum of Canada, Trenton, Ontario: *www.airforcemuseum.ca*.

Queen Mary Museum, Long Beach, California: *www.queenmary.com*.

Royal Canadian Air Force (Unofficial Site): *www.rcaf.com*.

Spitfire Emporium: *www.spitcrazy.com*.

Toronto Aerospace Museum: *www.torontoaerospacemuseum.com*.

Western Canada Aviation Museum, Winnipeg: *www.wcam.mb.ca*.

DATE DUE

FOLLETT

MARQUIS

Marquis Book Printing Inc.

Québec, Canada

2008